Last Poems

ALSO IN THIS SERIES

POETRY

Selected Poems

Adam / Adán (1916)
Square Horizon / Horizon carré (1917)
Equatorial & other poems (1917–18)
Arctic Poems / Poemas árticos (1918)
Painted Poems (1922 — unpublished) *
*Paris 1925: Ordinary Autumn & All of a Sudden /
      Automne régulier & Tout à coup* (1925)
Altazor (1931) *
Skyquake / Temblor de cielo (1931)
Citizen of Oblivion / El ciudadano del olvido (1941)
Seeing and Touching / Ver y palpar (1941)
Last Poems / Últimos poemas (1948)
Uncollected Poems / Poemas inéditos *

FICTION

El Cid / Mío Cid Campeador (1929)
Cagliostro (1934)
Three Huge Novels / Tres novelas inmensas [with Hans Arp] (1935)
Papa, or The Diary of Alicia Mir / Papa, o el diario de Alicia Mir (1934) *
Satyr, or The Power of Words / Sátiro, o el poder de la palabra (1939)

OTHER PROSE

Manifestos / Manifestes (1925)
Adverse Winds / Vientos contrarios (1926)

BIOGRAPHY

Volodia Teitelboim: *Vicente Huidobro — in perpetual motion: A Biography*

* Not yet published when this volume appeared.

Vicente Huidobro

Last Poems

Últimos poemas

Translated from Spanish by
Tony Frazer

Shearsman Books

First published in the United Kingdom in 2024 by
Shearsman Books Ltd
PO Box 4239
Swindon
SN3 9FN

Shearsman Books Ltd Registered Office
30–31 St. James Place, Mangotsfield, Bristol BS16 9JB
(this address not for correspondence)

www.shearsman.com

ISBN 978-1-84861-817-6

Translations copyright © Tony Frazer, 2024
Introduction and editorial matter copyright © Shearsman Books, 2024

The right of Tony Frazer to be identified as the translator of this work has been asserted by him in accordance with the Copyrights, Designs and Patents Act of 1988. All rights reserved.

The original texts of the poems in this volume are based on the first edition of *Últimos poemas* (Santiago: Talleres Gráficos Ahués Hnos., 1948), as well as on the texts printed in the author's *Obra poética* [Poetic Works], edited by Cedomil Goic (Paris: Éditions ALLCA XX, 2003). The text of the French language poem 'Le passager de son destin' is drawn from the first edition of the eponymous chapbook (Paris: Éditions Sagesse, au Librairie Tschann, 1937).

ACKNOWLEDGEMENTS
Some of the translations collected here appeared, in earlier versions, in Vicente Huidobro, *Selected Poems*, edited by Tony Frazer, with translations by Tony Frazer, Michael Smith & Luis Ingelmo, and Eliot Weinberger (Bristol: Shearsman Books, 2019).

As usual, I have needed to lean on the experience and knowledge of others from time to time when trying to wrestle these poems into English. I am especially grateful to Terence Dooley and to Jordi Doce for suggestions that saved me from some awkward errors. I've no doubt that others still remain, lurking in the background, and the fault for those are mine alone.

CONTENTS

	Introduction	7
14	El paso del retorno / Return Passage	15
24	Coronación de la muerte / Death's Coronation	25
28	Solitario invencible / Invincible Recluse	29
30	*Recuperar el cielo / Recovering the sky*	31
32	*La gran palabra / The great word*	33
34	Voz de esperanza / Voice of Hope	35
42	Hija / Daughter	43
44	Voz preferida / Favourite Voice	45
46	La vida es sueño / Life is a Dream	47
48	Aire de alba / Dawn Air	49
50	La poesía es un atentado celeste / Poetry is a Celestial Assault	51
52	La noche momentánea / The Fleeting Night	53
62	El hijo canta a la Madre Dolorosa / The Child Sings to Our Lady of Sorrows	63
66	Una tarde después del Rhin / One Evening Beyond the Rhine	67
70	*Días y noches te he buscado / Days and nights I have searched for you*	71
72	Quiero desaparecer y no morir / I want to disappear and not to die	73
74	*La noche viene a esperarse en mi / Night comes and puts its hopes in me*	75
76	Monumento al mar / Monument to the Sea	77
84	*Pienso en ellos en los muertos / I think of them I think of the dead*	85
86	*Tierra que te alimentas de mi tristeza / Land you feed on my sadness*	87
88	Alma seducida por su raza / Soul seduced by its lineage	89
90	*Te amo mujer de mi gran viaje / I love you woman from my great journey*	91
92	*Vagaba por las calles de una ciudad helada / I wandered the streets of a frozen city*	93
94	Ilusiones perdidas / Lost Illusions	95
96	*Una noche de campos profundos / A night of dense fields*	97
98	Exterior / Outside	99
100	*Ahora que mis ojos vuelan / Now that my eyes fly*	101

102	Edad negra / Dark Age	103
106	Madre / Mother	107
108	*Los labios pretenden alejarse de la boca /*	
	My lips try to leave my mouth	109
110	*Éramos los elegidos del sol / We were the chosen of the sun*	111
112	*Abramos nuestro pecho / Let us open our bosom*	113
114	Sea como sea / Be That As It May	115
118	*El año surcaba los aires / The year ploughed the air*	119
120	*Lejanía de murmullos / Remote murmurs*	121
122	Cambio al horizonte / Change of Horizon	123
126	De cuando en cuando / From Time to Time	127
128	Bellas promesas / Fine Promises	129
132	La mano del instante / The Hand at that Moment	133
134	Estrella hija de estrella / Star Child of Star	135
142	Palabras de la danza / Words from the Dance	143
146	Tiempo-Espacio / Time-Space	147
148	*Veo el universo reducido / I see the universe reduced*	149
152	El pasajero de su destino / Passenger of His Destiny	153
162	*La muerte que alguien espera / The death that someone awaits*	163

Appendix

166	Le passager de son destin / Passenger of His Destiny	167
174	La última entrevista: La colina del desencantado /	
	The Last Interview: The Disillusioned Man on the Hill	175

	Notes	192
	Textual Commentary	194

INTRODUCTION

Vicente Huidobro was born in Santiago de Chile in 1893; he died of a brain hæmorrhage in Cartagena, Chile on 2 January 1948, a few days before his fifty-fifth birthday.

Huidobro came from a wealthy patrician family. Unlike many youths of his age and class, Huidobro dedicated himself to literature. 'At the age of seventeen,' he was to write in 1926, 'I said to myself: "I have to be the leading poet in America"; then, as the years passed, I said: "I have to be the leading poet in my language"; finally, my ambitions soared and I said to myself: "I have to be the leading poet of my century".' Modesty was not one of Huidobro's defining characteristics.

After some early literary successes and the publication of several books, Huidobro left Chile with his family in late 1916, bound first for Madrid, and then for Paris. While he very much wanted to see what was happening in the world's artistic capital, the initial impetus for the move had in fact been the avoidance of further scandal at home, from which Huidobro had not long before disappeared to Buenos Aires with Teresa Wilms Montt (1893–1921). The pair certainly had an affair, but the event also had a somewhat more gentlemanly aspect, as Huidobro had engineered Teresa's escape from the Santiago convent in which she had been immured by her irate husband, following her affair with one of his cousins. Teresa was to develop her own literary career in Buenos Aires and would later move on to Europe, where she was to commit suicide in 1921. Huidobro continued to remember her long afterwards, and the daring escape to Argentina prefigured his later exploits with Ximena Amunátegui, who was to become his second, albeit common-law wife.

In Paris he threw himself into the artistic avant-garde, participating in (and part-financing) a Cubist magazine, *Nord-Sud*, edited by Pierre Reverdy and establishing friendships with Juan Gris, Picasso, Picabia and Lipchitz, as well as with poets such as Apollinaire, Cendrars and Cocteau. In July of 1918, to escape the war, he moved to Madrid where he participated in the *tertulia* (literary salon) of Ramón Gómez de la Serna at the Café Pombo; he also came into contact there with rising young writers such as Gerardo Diego, Jorge Luis Borges and Juan Larrea. During this febrile period he published two full-sized collections of poetry and four chapbooks, half of them in Spanish and half in French.

In 1918 Huidobro was obliged to return to Chile for his sister's wedding. He hoped to take literary Santiago by storm, but instead he met with a blank wall of conservatism and indifference. He returned to Paris in 1920 and, in 1921, published a selected poems, *Saisons choisies* [Selected Seasons], accompanied by a statement of his own aesthetic principles, 'La Création pure'. But Huidobro's Creationism – a kind of literary cubism, which argued for the independence of artistic works from empirical reality – was soon overtaken by Surrealism and the craze for automatic writing, which he rejected as 'the reduction of poetry to a simple, after-dinner, family pastime'. Creationism was a useful label, a marketing slogan in modern terms, under which attention was sought, and gained. As is still the case today, commentators happily discussed the supposedly attendant theories rather than the works that exemplified them.

In 1925, political changes in Chile attracted his attention and Huidobro, always thinking in the grandest terms, saw an opportunity to become the political leader of a new Chile. Even his mother had contemplated her son as King Vicente I of Chile. The (pipe)dream of a Huidobro monarchy, however, was not to be realised. In 1925 he also issued two further collections of poetry in French, *Automne régulier* [Ordinary Autumn] and *Tout à coup* [All of a Sudden], two experimental dead-ends, which show him toying with Dada and Surrealism, although more positive signs of development were in fact to be found as, during the same period, he began to publish sections from the work-in-progress, *Altazor*, in Spanish, in literary journals.

Huidobro had married young, to Manuela Portales Bello (1894–1965), likewise the scion of an upper-crust family, with whom he had four children and from whom he later separated to form a new and scandalous relationship with the sixteen-year-old Ximena Amunátegui (1910–1975), with whom he would go on to have a fifth child. The beginnings of this relationship, in which, after meeting her at a costume ball, Huidobro published a long love poem, 'Pasión y muerte' [Passion and Death] in Santiago's *La Nación* newspaper on Good Friday, obliged Huidobro to leave Chile, first for Paris, then for New York in 1927 where he came close to becoming involved in the film business. He met Douglas Fairbanks and Gloria Swanson, and even won a prize of US$10,000 (ca. $150,000 in today's dollars) for his film-script, *Cagliostro* – later converted into a novella – as being the best candidate for a new movie. Nothing came of this, because of the arrival of the *talkies* shortly afterwards, which immediately rendered the expressionist silent style of *Cagliostro* out of date.

Huidobro's former colleagues in the Parisian avant-garde evidently saw the furore over a teenage paramour, and an abortive presidential campaign,

as signs of madness, or, at the very least early-onset mid-life crisis. It is not clear what they thought of the press photos of Huidobro with Hollywood starlets, although one can hazard a guess.

When Ximena reached her majority in 1928, Huidobro left New York and travelled secretly to Chile where he scooped her up from outside her convent school – as a subterfuge, she had sought permission from the nuns to go to the dentist – and the pair fled to Argentina. A former family maid had acted as go-between for the pair. Within a few months the couple reappeared in Paris where they were allegedly married in a Muslim ceremony, the only procedure that would legalise their union. In the following years in Paris Huidobro completed his two major works, *Altazor* and *Temblor de cielo* [Skyquake] – although the author claimed that parts of the former date back as far as 1919 – as well as the novel *Mío Cid Campeador* (available in this series under the title *El Cid*).

In 1932 economic realities necessitated Huidobro's return to Chile. Politically at this time, he was a man of the Left, although in the 1940s he would become a militant anti-Communist. At the outbreak of the Spanish Civil War, Huidobro organised Chilean intellectuals in support of the Republic and in 1937 he was in Spain, with Líster's troops on the Aragón front, and took part in literary conferences in Madrid and Valencia.

By the early 1940s, however, Huidobro was thoroughly disillusioned with politics, which he described as 'the art of lying, of concealing, of falsifying, of dirtying life, of buying and selling consciences'. He was also deeply affected by the death of his mother, by the fall of France, and then by the collapse of his second 'marriage': Ximena had found new love with a younger suitor, the Argentine-born poet and architect Godofredo Iommi (1917–2001), going on to marry him after her separation from Huidobro – a divorce not being required as her union with Vicente had no legal standing.

Escaping this situation, Huidobro went to France in 1944 as a war correspondent for newspapers in Montevideo and Buenos Aires and was with Allied troops in Germany, even broadcasting from Paris on The Voice of America. During the war Huidobro was wounded twice and was obliged to go to London for medical treatment. When at last in 1945 he returned to Chile it was with a new partner, Raquel Señoret (1922–1990), who had previously been married to an English writer and was the daughter of the late Chilean Ambassador to the United Kingdom. The couple set up home in Cartagena, a coastal resort south of Valparaíso. In the short time left to him, Huidobro took little interest in contemporary Chilean poetry.

* * *

The above summary of Vicente Huidobro's life does little justice to one of the most flamboyant, gifted and relentlessly innovative poets of the 20th century. He had the grandest notion of the function of the poet, and did his best to live up to it. His literary presence is still felt in Latin American poetry and, as with his contemporary, the great Peruvian poet, César Vallejo, there is a growing appreciation of his work in the English-speaking world. His poetry is wonderfully experimental, sometimes outrageous, narcissistic, and egotistical in a quasi-Whitmanesque fashion, but it constitutes a splendid corrective to our sometimes lazy view of the trajectory of 20th-century poetry. It is my firm conviction that, warts and all, Huidobro is one of the defining figures of 20th century Hispanic poetry.

* * *

This volume is the first complete English translation of the book that was assembled by Huidobro's eldest daughter, Manuela, after his death, and published just a few months later. I believe, although I have seen no definitive statement to this effect, that Eduardo Anguita – editor of Huidobro's *Antología* (1945), and a close friend and long-time supporter of the author – probably helped Manuela in her labours.

In his final years, Huidobro had mentioned to friends – among them, Juan Larrea – his plans for new collections of poetry: *Sin días y sin noches* [Without Days and Without Nights]; *Utilidad de las estrellas* [Usefulness of the Stars] – which was also mentioned as the title of a prose book; *El precio del alba* [The Price of Dawn] – announced as forthcoming both in Paris and in Montevideo. Of the latter, Huidobro said,

> Estos poemas muestran el precio que yo he pagado –y que fue casi mi vida– por un renacimiento espiritual completo, por la plenitud, por la renovación absoluta de mi ser.*

> [These poems show the price I have paid – and it almost cost me my life – for a complete spiritual rebirth, for repletion, for the absolute renewal of my being.]

---

* In an interview with Jorge Onfray, 'La colina del desencantado' [The Disillusioned Man on the Hill], *Zig-Zag*, Santiago, 26 September, 1946. A full translation of this interview may be found in the appendix to this volume.

The posthumous publication certainly contains some work that the author had intended for one or other of these planned books, as well as a number of uncollected poems that had previously appeared in magazines, a few occasional poems – such as those occasioned by the German invasion of France – together with several manuscripts that had not been published in any form, these including stray untitled pieces that appear, in many cases, to be unfinished poems, or texts that might perhaps have been incorporated in longer works had the author lived longer. It is thus something of a mixed bag, but still contains valuable work that all admirers of the poet will be glad to have, including some of the most significant of his late poems. Works such as 'El paso del retorno', 'La poesía es un atentado celeste', 'Monumento al mar' and 'El pasajero de su destino' are all important texts that sit comfortably alongside the finest of the author's later poems, and I have long felt that his later works are far more important than they have generally been given credit for. The texts have been sequenced in accordance with the first edition – a PDF of which is available for download from the Biblioteca Nacional de Chile – but their layouts and orthography mostly follow the *Obra poética* (2003), a scholarly edition, while reference has also been made to the 2021 collected edition, *Poesía reunida*. The reason for this is that the first edition contains a number of obvious errors and, it would appear, some editorial interventions, above all in the matter of punctuation. I have thus regarded the 2003 texts to be the safer master versions – apart from the issue of full left-justification of carried-over long lines – with double-checks against the 2021 edition in cases of doubt. The Appendix contains one French text – Huidobro's own French version of the poem, 'El pasajero de su destino' – and, at the end, I have added the author's final interview for good measure.

Other poems not in this volume, and which had previously been collected in the 1945 *Antología*, a Selected Poems edited by Eduardo Anguita and published in Santiago, plus some further stray poems – including further occasional works – will be found in the final volume in this series, *Uncollected Poems*, a volume which will be almost as long as this one.

The notes at the end of the book explain the provenance of the texts, and some specific textual issues.

Tony Frazer
July 2024

Depositaria, por voluntad expresa de mi padre, de todos sus manuscritos, no he querido dilatar por más tiempo la publicación de aquellos poemas que constituyen su obra inédita.

He creído oportuno, eso se agregar algunos de sus poemas ya aparecidos en revistas, para que, de este modo, se pueda apreciar en su conjunto todo el trabajo poético de su madurez.

A la Memoria de mi padre adorado dedico este trabajo, hecho con inmensa ternura y veneración.

Manuela Huidobro de Yrarrázaval

As the trustee, according to my father's specific wishes, of all his manuscripts, I did not wish to delay any longer the publication of those poems which make up his unpublished work.

I thought it appropriate to add some of his poems that have already appeared in magazines, so that his entire mature poetic work can thus be appreciated as a whole.

I dedicate this work, created with the greatest tenderness and reverence, to the Memory of my beloved father.

MANUELA HUIDOBRO DE YRARRÁZAVAL

EL PASO DEL RETORNO

Yo soy ése que salió hace un año de su tierra
Buscando lejanías de vida y muerte
Su propio corazón y el corazón del mundo
Cuando el viento silbaba entrañas
En un crepúsculo gigante y sin recuerdos

Guiado por mi estrella
Con el pecho vacío
Y los ojos clavados en la altura
Salí hacia mi destino

Oh mis buenos amigos
Me habéis reconocido
He vivido una vida que no puede vivirse
Pero tú Poesía no me has abandonado un solo instante

Oh mis amigos aquí estoy
Vosotros sabéis acaso lo que yo era
Pero nadie sabe lo que soy

El viento me hizo viento
La sombra me hizo sombra
El horizonte me hizo horizonte preparado a todo
La tarde me hizo tarde
Y el alba me hizo alba para cantar de nuevo

Oh poeta esos tremendos ojos
Ese andar de alma de acero y de bondad de mármol
Este es aquel que llegó al final del último camino
Y que vuelve quizás con otro paso
Hago al andar el ruido de la muerte
Y si mis ojos os dicen
Cuánta vida he vivido y cuánta muerte he muerto

RETURN PASSAGE

I am the one who left his homeland a year ago
Seeking distance from life and death
His own heart and the heart of the world
When the wind was whistling to its core
At nightfall and with no memories

Guided by my star
With an empty breast
And my eyes fixed on the heights
I left for my destiny

Oh my good friends
Did you recognise me
I have lived a life that cannot be lived
But you Poetry you have not abandoned me for one single moment

Oh my friends here I am
You know perhaps what I was
But no-one knows what I am

The wind made me wind
The shadow made me shadow
The horizon made me horizon and ready for anything
The evening made me evening
And the dawn made me dawn so that I might sing once again

Oh poet those terrible eyes
That steel-souled manner with a marmoreal kindness
This is the man who reached the end of the final path
And who returns perhaps in another guise
I walk along with a death rattle in my throat
And if my eyes tell you
How much life I have lived and how much death I have died

Ellos podrían también deciros
Cuánta vida he muerto y cuánta muerte he vivido

Oh mis fantasmas Oh mis queridos espectros
La noche ha dejado noche en mis cabellos
En dónde estuve por dónde he andado
Pero era ausencia aquélla o era mayor presencia

Cuando las piedras oyen mi paso
Sienten une ternura que les ensancha el alma
Se hacen señas furtivas y hablan bajo
Allí se acerca el buen amigo
El hombre de las distancias
Que viene fatigado de tanta muerte al hombro
De tanta vida en el pecho
Y busca donde pasar la noche

Heme aquí ante vuestros limpios ojos
Heme aquí vestido de lejanías
Atrás quedaron los negros nubarrones
Los años de tinieblas en el antro olvidado
Traigo un alma lavada por el fuego
Vosotros me llamáis sin saber a quién llamáis
Traigo un cristal sin sombra un corazón que no decae
La imagen de la nada y un rostro que sonríe
Traigo un amor muy parecido al universo
La Poesía me despejó el camino
Ya no hay banalidades en mi vida
Quién guió mis pasos de modo tan certero

Mis ojos dicen a aquéllos que cayeron
Disparad contra mi vuestros dardos
Vengad en mí vuestras angustias
Vengad en mi vuestros fracasos
Yo soy invulnerable
He tomado mi sitio en el cielo como el silencio

They could tell you too
How much life I have died and how much death I have lived

Oh my phantoms Oh my dear wraiths
The night has left night in my hair
Where have I been where have I wandered
But was that really absence or was it a greater presence

When the stones hear my footsteps
They feel a tenderness that swells their souls
They make furtive signs and speak softly
Over there a good friend approaches
A man from far-off lands
Who arrives weary with so much death on his shoulders
With so much life in his breast
Seeking a place to spend the night

Here I am before your innocent eyes
Here I am clothed in distance
Gone are the black storm clouds
Years of darkness in forgotten caverns
I bear a soul cleansed by fire
You call to me without knowing whom you call
I bear a crystal with no shadow a heart which does not weaken
The image of nothingness and a smiling face
I bear a love very much like the universe
Poetry cleared the way for me
There are no longer banalities in my life
Who guided my steps in such a sure fashion

My eyes say to those who fell
Fire your darts at me
Avenge your distress upon me
Avenge your disasters upon me
I am invulnerable
Like the silence I have taken my place in the heavens

Los siglos de la tierra me caen en los brazos
Yo soy amigos el viajero sin fin

Las alas de la enorme aventura
Batían entre inviernos y veranos
Mirad cómo suben estrellas en mi alma
Desde que he expulsado las serpientes del tiempo oscurecido

Cómo podremos entendernos
Heme aquí de regreso de donde no se vuelve
Compasión de las olas y piedad de los astros
Cuánto tiempo perdido
Este es el hombre de las lejanías
El que daba vuelta las páginas de los muertos
Sin tiempo sin espacio sin corazón sin sangre
El que andaba de un lado para otro
Desesperado y solo en las tinieblas
Solo en el vacío
Como un perro que ladra hacia el fondo de un abismo

Oh vosotros Oh mis buenos amigos
Los que habéis tocado mis manos
Qué habéis tocado
Y vosotros que habéis escuchado mi voz
Qué habéis escuchado
Y los que habéis contemplado mis ojos
Qué habéis contemplado

Lo he perdido todo y todo lo he ganado
Y ni siquiera pido
La parte de la vida que me corresponde
Ni montañas de fuego ni mares cultivados
Es tanto más lo que he ganado que lo que he perdido
Así es el viajo al fin del mundo

Y ésta es la corona de sangre de la gran experiencia
La corona regalo de mi estrella
En dónde estuve en dónde estoy

The ages of the earth fall into my arms
My friends I am the eternal traveller

The wings of the great adventure
Flap between winters and summers
Watch how stars rise in my soul
Ever since I expelled the serpents of darker times

How will we be able to understand one other
Here I am back again from that place of no return
Compassion of waves and mercy of stars
How much time has been lost
This is the man from distant lands
The man who turned the pages of the dead
With no time no space no heart no blood
The man who wandered from one place to another
Desperate and alone in the darkness
Alone in the void
Like a dog barking at the bottom of an abyss

Oh you Oh my good friends
Those of you who touched my hands
What did you touch
And you who heard my voice
What did you hear
And you who observed my eyes
What did you observe

I have lost everything and I have gained everything
And I do not even ask for
The share of life that I deserve
Neither mountains of fire nor cultivated seas
What I have gained is so much more than I have lost
Such is the journey to the end of the world

And this is the crown of blood from that great experience
The crown bestowed by my star
Where was I where am I

Los árboles lloran un pájaro canta inconsolable
Decid quién es el muerto
El viento me solloza qué inquietudes me has dado
Algunas flores exclaman
Estás vivo aún
Quién es el muerto entonces
Las aguas gimen tristemente
Quién ha muerto en estas tierras

Ahora sé lo que soy y lo que era
Conozco la distancia que va del hombre a la verdad
Conozco la palabra que aman los muertos
Éste es el que ha llorado el mundo el que ha llorado resplandores
Las lágrimas se hinchan se dilatan
Y empiezan a girar sobre su eje
Heme aquí ante vosotros
Cómo podremos entendernos cómo saber lo que decimos
Hay tantos muertos que me llaman
Allí donde la tierra pierde su ruido
Allí donde me esperan mis queridos fantasmas
Mis queridos espectros
Miradme os amo tanto pero soy extranjero
Quien salió de su tierra
Sin saber el hondor de su aventura
Al desplegar las alas
El mismo no sabía qué vuelo era su vuelo

Vuestro tiempo y vuestro espacio
No son mi espacio ni mi tiempo
Quién es el extranjero Reconocéis su andar
Es el que vuelve con un sabor de eternidad en la garganta
Con un olor de olvido en los cabellos
Con un sonar de venas misteriosas
Es éste que está llorando el universo
Que sobrepasó la muerte y el rumor de la selva secreta
Soy impalpable ahora como ciertas semillas
Que el viento mismo que las lleva no las siente
Oh Poesía nuestro reino empieza

The trees weep a bird sings inconsolably
Tell me who is the dead man
The wind sobs at me what worries you have brought me
Some flowers exclaim
Are you still alive
Who then is the dead man
The waters moan sadly
Who has died in these lands

Now I know what I am and what I was
I know the distance between man and truth
I know the word loved by the dead
This is the man who wept for the world the one who wept for the light
Tears well up they keep flowing
And start to turn on their axis
Here I stand before you
How can we understand one another how can we know what we say
There are so many of the dead calling out to me
Over there where the earth loses its sound
Over there my beloved phantoms await me
My beloved wraiths
Look at me I love you all so much but I am a stranger
Who left his homeland
Without knowing where his adventures would take him
When unfolding his wings
Even he did not know what kind of flight his would be

Your time and your space
Are not my space not my time
Who is this stranger   Do you recognise the way he walks
He is the one returning with a taste of eternity in his throat
With the smell of oblivion in his hair
With the sound of mysterious veins
He is the one mourning the universe
Who went beyond death and the murmurs of the secret forest
I am intangible now like those seeds
That the wind cannot sense even though it carries them
Oh Poetry this is the start of our reign

Este es aquél que durmió muchas veces
Allí donde hay que estar alerta
Donde las rocas prohíben la palabra
Allí donde se confunde la muerte con el canto del mar
Ahora vengo a saber que fui a buscar las llaves
He aquí las llaves
Quién las había perdido
Cuánto tiempo ha que se perdieron
Nadie encontró las llaves perdidas en el tiempo y en las brumas
Cuántos siglos perdidas

Al fondo de las tumbas
Al fondo de los mares
Al fondo del murmullo de los vientos
Al fondo del silencio
He aquí los signos
Cuánto tiempo olvidados
Pero entonces amigo qué vas a decirnos
Quién ha de comprenderte De dónde vienes
En dónde estabas En qué alturas en qué profundidades
Andaba por la Historia del brazo con la muerte

Oh hermano nada voy a decirte
Cuando hayas tocado lo que nadie puede tocar
Más que el árbol te gustaría callar

This is the man who slept many times
There where vigilance is required
Where the rocks forbid speech
There where death is confused with the song of the sea
Now I realise I went in search of the keys
Here are the keys
Who lost them
How long have they been lost
No-one found the keys lost in time and in the mists
Lost for how many centuries

Deep in the tombs
Deep in the sea
Deep in the murmuring winds
Deep in the silence
Here are the signs
How long forgotten
But then friend   what are you going to tell us
Who will understand you   Where do you come from
Where were you How high did you go how deep
I wandered through History arm in arm with death

Oh brother I will never tell you
When you have touched what no-one can touch
Even more than the trees you would rather remain silent

CORONACIÓN DE LA MUERTE

Moría una paloma bajo los grandes árboles del mundo
Cuán amargo es el aire de los países que desfilan
Las nubes te despiden entre pequeñas lágrimas en busca de un apoyo
     celeste
Moría la rosa en su temblante pedestal   Cuánta leyenda cantada por
     las tardes en diversos tonos
El llanto se esparcía por las piezas oscuras
Moría la flor-paloma y el hijo ponía su dolor en el pecho del mundo
Se iba la flor-paloma por el aire y un gran silencio caía en los caminos

Yo quiero hablaros de los ojos de la muerte   Del suspiro postrero
De las maneras de morir tan distintas como los andares
Hijo qué haces de tu dolor los meses van a venir los años las primaveras
Cortejo de sol y estrellas con tanto espíritu y variadas voces
He puesto mi alma en ese último suspiro y por lo tanto qué ha de ser
     de mí
Tierra sin árboles corazón sin hierbas ni palomas
Como puedes andar entre esperanzas ajenas
Qué voz solemne ha salido de su almendra   Qué canto es ése que era
     el mío y desconozco
El mar se llena de alma y las rosas escuchan y las arenas no saben que
     hacer ni que decir
Así se muere   Un airecillo leve entre los dientes un temblor en los
     pétalos un reflejo de rocío extrahumano en los cabellos dolorosos
     y resignados
Qué voz solemne viene entrando en este árbol de memoria frágil como
     el humo y las cuerdas del arpa
Qué llanto milenario de tribus en la noche y de edades perdidas enlaza
     los pechos de los siglos
Qué alarido de buscadores de fortunas asesinados en los bosques oscuros
Qué sollozo de sueño horrendo bajo el techo caído de repente

DEATH'S CORONATION

A dove died under the world's great trees
How bitter the atmosphere is in those countries marching past
The clouds bid you farewell in little teardrops seeking celestial support
The rose died on its shaking pedestal   How many legends sung of an evening in various keys
Mourning spread through the dark rooms
The flower-dove died and the child placed his pain inside the world's breast
The flower-dove flew through the air and a great silence fell upon the roads

I want to tell you about the eyes of death   Of the final breath
Of ways of dying as different as ways of walking
Child what will you do with your pain in the coming months years springtimes
Procession of sun and stars with so much spirit and mixed voices
I have put my soul into that final breath and so what is to become of me
Land with no trees heart with no herbs no doves
How can you walk amongst the hopes of others
What a solemn voice emerged from its kernel   What song is that which once was mine and now I do not recognise
The sea is full of soul and the roses listen and the sands know not what to do nor what to say
So it is that one dies   A puff of breath between the teeth a tremor in the petals a reflection of superhuman dew in agonising and acquiescent hair
What a solemn voice comes into this tree of memory fragile as smoke and harp strings
What ancient mourning by tribes in the night and in ages long gone links the breasts of centuries
What shrieking by fortune seekers murdered in the dark woods
What sobbing in horrid dreams under a roof that suddenly fell in

La sonrisa era cosa del alba
La otra orilla de la amargura El tiempo de las semillas trae un brillo en sus espadas una capa de gloria sobre los hombros
La sonrisa era cosa de magnolia era cosa de ropas lavándose en el río entre espumas
La sonrisa era cosa de frutas y ventanas abiertas   Era cosa de colores disparados al sol
Oh suspiro de los muertes Oh alma hija de mis rosas Oh flor-paloma por qué me has deshojado al deshojarte
Llega el suspiro Todo es inútil Oh viento del otro lado tan ansioso de su sitio Se fue se va el suspiro
Y yo me voy con él empujando las puertas de la muerte

The smile had something of the dawn
The other side of bitterness The sowing season brings a brightness to their swords a cloak of glory across their shoulders
The smile had something of magnolia it had something of clothes washed in the river amongst the spray
The smile had something of fruit and open windows It had something of colours fired at the sun
O breath of the dead O daughter soul of my roses Oh flower-dove why did you shed my leaves when you shed yours
Breath comes Everything is futile O wind from the other side so eager for its place It has gone the breath is leaving
And I go with it pushing at the gates of death

SOLITARIO INVENCIBLE

Resbalando
Como canasta de amarguras
Con mucho silencio y mucha luz
Dormido de hielos
Te vas y vuelves a ti mismo
Te ríes de tu propio sueño
Pero suspiras poemas temblorosos
Y te convences de alguna esperanza

La ausencia el hambre de callar
De no emitir más tantas hipótesis
De cerrar las heridas habladoras
Te da una ansia especial
Como de nieve y fuego
Quieres volver los ojos a la vida
Tragarte el universo entero
Esos campos de estrellas
Se te van de la mano después de la catástrofe
Cuando el perfume de los claveles
Gira en torno de su eje

INVINCIBLE RECLUSE

Sliding along
Like a basket of bitterness
With a lot of silence and a lot of light
Sleeping on ice
You go away and come back to yourself
You laugh at your own dream
But you exhale trembling poems
And you convince yourself you have some hope

The absence the hunger to keep quiet
To stop circulating so many theories
To close the speaking wounds
Gives you a special craving
Like snow and fire
You want to turn your eyes back towards life
Swallow the whole universe
Those fields of stars
They fall from your hand after the catastrophe
When the scent of carnations
Revolves around its axis

[RECUPERAR EL CIELO]

Recuperar el cielo
Recuperar la tierra
Envolver el mundo en ritmos de experiencia
Aprisionar el éter que se escapa
Aprisionar el aire
Con esta carne presurosa
En olas envolventes sobre el ensueño
Y la fuga de las estrellas en el momento en que iban a contar su historia

[RECOVERING THE SKY]

Recovering the sky
Recovering the land
Wrapping the world in experienced rhythms
Imprisoning the escaping ether
Imprisoning the air
With this nimble flesh
In all-embracing waves over the daydream
And the stars escaping just when they were about to tell their story

[LA GRAN PALABRA]

La gran palabra
Lázaro ¿la has olvidado?
El mar dobla su vida
Año de gloria las águilas dominan sin impaciencia
La enorme mano escribe
El mundo tiene aún su pequeña esperanza
Hospital que renace de sus cenizas cada día
La palabra olvidada te dejó olvidada
Ven a mi pecho a tomar armonía

Murmullo del vacío
Tu cabeza redobla y llena el cielo

Alfabeto perdido por los siglos
Sobre las montañas y los campos
La paz que viene como una carta
Especial para la esfinge

Los que bajan la escalera de la muerte
Y los que van en compañía de sus estatuas
Por los caminos sin historia
Oh cuántos laberintos venidos a menos
En los mundos de ayer a causa de sus monstruos

[THE GREAT WORD]

The great word
Lazarus did you forget it?
The sea doubles its life
Year of glory the eagles rule without impatience
The enormous hand writes
The world still retains a little hope
Hospital that is reborn from its ashes every day
The forgotten word left you forgotten
Come to my breast to capture harmony

Murmur from the void
Your head tilts back and fills the sky

Alphabet lost for centuries
On mountains and fields
Peace that comes like a letter
Specifically for the sphinx

Those who descend the ladder of death
And those who go accompanied by their statues
On roads with no history
Oh how many down-at-heel labyrinths
In the worlds of yesterday because of their monsters

VOZ DE ESPERANZA

Tienes ojos de orgullo desesperado y de fuego cubierto
Tienes carne color tormento milenario como los desiertos
De cólera variada y en el fondo idéntica
Tu tristeza es sentir la injusticia vertiginosa que enmohece la marcha
Y arrastra los pedazos
Tu dicha sería romper las ataduras que te llaman a las tinieblas
Y crear con tus manos un planeta en forma de corazón

Oyes la tos de los esclavos y un horno ruge en tus entrañas
Oyes las maldiciones abatidas
Oyes gemir y gimes
Con todo tu esqueleto de amarguras inmensas
Oyes los gritos del hambre bajo sombreros como tabacos deshojados
Bajo los harapos de nocturnas facturas
Oyes el llanto y lloras
Oyes la muerte que sale de la noche entrando en los huesos
Oyes el cuerpo del mundo repartido en lamentos
Oyes al angustiado hermano de los pechos sin aire
Oyes gemir y gimes
Mojado de siglos y catástrofes mojado de esperanzas
Oyes la súplica de los mares empuñados
Oyes caer las lágrimas a lo largo de la noche
Y las ves atravesar el día
Oyes sufrir y sufres
Oyes llorar al hombre y lloras como el hombre

Pero una fiebre de mariposa gigantesca
Parto del alba retardada entre redes opacas
Nace una hoguera y nace una voz rodeado de fuego
Una voz que redime a un astro ciego y taciturno
Una voz que se ha lavado en largos sueños

VOICE OF HOPE

You have eyes of desperate pride filled with fire
You have flesh the colour of age-old torment like deserts
Of assorted rage and in the exact same background
Your sadness lies in feeling the dizzying injustice that makes progress rusty
And sweeps the shards away
It would be your good fortune to break the ties that summon you to the
    darkness
And create a heart-shaped planet with your hands

You hear slaves coughing and a furnace roars in your vitals
You hear curses cast down
You hear groaning and you groan
With your entire skeleton of immense bitterness
You hear cries of hunger under hats like tobacco plants stripped of their
    leaves
Under the rags of night
You hear weeping and you weep
You hear death emerging from the night entering bones
You hear the body of the world divided into laments
You hear the anguished brother with airless lungs
You hear groaning and you groan
Damp with centuries and catastrophes damp with hope
You hear the plea of the clenched seas
You hear tears falling throughout the night
And you see them penetrate the day
You hear suffering and you suffer
You hear a man weeping and you weep like a man

But a monstrous butterfly fever
Delayed birth of dawn amongst opaque nets
A bonfire is born and a voice is born surrounded by fire
A voice that redeems a blind taciturn star
A voice that has been washed in long dreams

Una voz de torrente sacudido
Una voz de pavorosas profundidades
Una voz que levanta los gestos
Blandiendo el mundo entre centellas iracundas
Martillando en la fragua del universo
Una voz cansada de llorar
Y que se alza de sus principios
A la dignidad negada por inmundas razones
Y exigida por todas las raíces de su ser invencible
Una voz cansada de gemir

El hombre es paciente
Pero no tanto como el tiempo contemplado
Desde la orilla de la noche
El hombre es sufrido
Sus músculos labrados a golpes de milenios
Pero la tierra es suave y le comprende y le ama
De tantos siglos hasta tantos
El hombre es afable
La tierra le ama y pide un modo de armonía
Y quiere una forma de fraterna dulzura
No quiere estar cubierta de tragedias
Ni rodar bajo crímenes entre fiebres sangrientas
La tierra le ama
(Que sea siempre así)
Quiere su luz de flor meditativa
Quiere su dicha como un canto necesario a la marcha
Que caigan entonces los que construyen la desgracia
Los que cierran el horizonte
Los que impiden el canto
Que se entierren al fondo de su noche
Que caigan sí que caigan
Y vamos descargando los muertos al borde del planeta
Arrojemos carroñas al vacío
Y que el cometa del mal agüero les envuelva en su sudario
Y los arrastre a la nada sin memoria

A flood-tossed voice
A voice from the dreadful depths
A voice that makes gestures
Wielding the world amongst angry sparks
Hammering in the forge of the universe
A voice tired of weeping
And which rises from its principles
To dignity denied for dishonest reasons
And demanded by all the roots of its invincible being
A voice tired of groaning

The man is patient
But not as much as the weather viewed
From the shores of night
The man is long-suffering
His muscles carved by the blows of the ages
But the earth is soft and understands him has loved him
For so many centuries and will for many more
The man is good-natured
The earth loves him and begs a kind of harmony
And wants a kind of fraternal sweetness
It does not want to be decked in tragedy
Nor exist under crimes amidst bloody fevers
The earth loves him
(May it always be so)
Wants its meditative flower light
Wants its bliss like songs required for marching
Let those fall who cause misfortune
Those who close the horizon
Those who block the song
Let them be buried in the depths of their night
Let them fall yes let them fall
And we are unloading the dead onto the planet's shores
Let us throw carrion into the void
And may the comet of ill omen wrap them in its shroud
And drag them into the void where there is no memory

Se acercan los hombres en marcha desprendida
De montañas geológicas y llenos de ternura
Viene el hombre amado de la tierra
Con sus ojos de abrazo suficiente
Llega el hombre a pedir sus derechos
Yo me descubro a tu paso como ante un mar
Que viene de la noche
Y te entrego mis manos y te entrego mi pecho
Y dejo a tus plantas la actitud de mi cerebro

Tienes un cuerpo traspasado como alarido de perro nebuloso
Tienes tu voz de lágrima a sonrisa
Tienes tu cielo como un mar levantado por sus ansias
Tu tristeza es ver que no saben lo que valen bajo tu piel terrestre
Tu alegría amasar el futuro de tus hijos como hierbas entusiastas
De tu mujer como árbol de dulzura

Arboles árboles velad sobre el destino
Arboles cantando su existencia
Sed luminosos sobre el sueño del aprecio

Qué hora sería en el revés del mundo
Cuando tu corazón sintió su hora
Y que tu piel terrestre fue traspasada de alaridos
Arboles árboles qué desnudez se acerca
Y qué mañanas de metal cantante se preparan
Las hojas contaban a la tierra sus proezas
Y la visión del venidero ilustre se alzó en algunos ojos exclusivos
Que desde entonces lloran de fiebre entusiasmada

Qué hora sería qué hora
Cuando el mundo te trajo la noticia del futuro coronado
Los pies se hicieron rápidos
El cuerpo se vistió de desnudez en estatuas de viento
Y los ojos devorándose entre ellos como dos locos furibundos
Rodaron entre soles y vidrios por todo el universo

Men approach in loose formation
From geological mountains and full of tenderness
The man beloved of the earth comes
With suitably embracing eyes
The man arrives demanding his rights
I discover myself in your wake as if before a sea
That arrives out of the night
And I give you my hands and I give you my breast
And I leave my frame of mind to your plants

Your body is penetrated as if by the howling of misty dogs
Your voice carries tears and smiles
Your sky is like a sea elevated by its longings
Your sadness lies in seeing they don't know their own worth under your
    earthly skin
Your pleasure in preparing your children's future like enthusiastic herbs
Or your wife's like a tree of delights

Trees trees you must watch over fate
Trees singing of their existence
Shine brightly on the dream of respect

What time would it be on the other side of the world
When your heart felt its time had come
And your earthly skin was pierced by screams
Trees trees what nakedness approaches
And what singing metal mornings are brewing
The leaves told the earth of their exploits
And the vision of an illustrious future arose in a few exclusive eyes
Since when they have wept in an excited fever

What time would it be what time
When the world brought you news of the crowned future
Your feet moved faster
Your body's nakedness was clad with statues of wind
And your eyes devouring each other like two furious madmen
Orbited amongst suns and windows throughout the universe

Tus manos qué delirio de fuego qué ancha simpatía
Qué lento abrazo a los ruidos de la vida
Tu corazón en buzo bajando a sus raíces
Nadando en sus comienzos   De pie en su objeto comprendido
Tenías tanta hambre de ti mismo

Ruta de oscuras geologías de selvas submarinas
Y de sombras arrodilladas bajo el viento
Hasta el momento que una tiza en el sueño trazó el destino
Levantó los gestos de sus profundidades
Y te dijo lo que eras y tendrías que ser
Sobre ese pedestal que recorres inconsciente

Qué hora sería qué hora cayendo de los árboles
Cuando los muertos dieron la orden de despertar

Y les tribus soñolientas mirando las estrellas
Se pusieron en marcha hacia las formas de sus lenguas
Hacia su esencia de memorias desveladas
Y su pasión de ser en penetrante vida
Idea redentora como un pan oscuro que se hace luz de sangre y células
Qué hora sería entonces
El huracán rugía entre sus barbas sorprendido
Y el viaje era una estatua de su raíz al tronco y al ramaje
Un trabajo invisible de siglos y cimientos anhelantes de aire
No hay detención posible hasta el arco de flores y horizontes
Que señala tu triunfo

Es el hombre
El hombre de pie sobre sus sueños

Your hands what delusions of fire what broad sympathies
What a slow embrace for the sounds of life
Your heart a diver going down to its roots
Swimming at the beginning   Standing upright at its intended target
You were so hungry for yourself

Path of dark geologies of undersea forests
And of shadows kneeling beneath the wind
Until the moment a piece of chalk in the dream marked out the destination
Made gestures from the depths
And told you what you were and what you would have to be
On that pedestal that you unconsciously travel around

What would the time be what time falling from the trees
When the dead gave the order to awake

And the sleepy tribes observing the stars
Set out on the road to the forms of their language
To the essence of unveiled memories
And their passion for existing in thrilling life
A redemptive idea like dark bread that turns blood and cells into light
What would the time be then
Surprised the hurricane roared through its remains
And the journey was a statue from root to trunk and to its branches
An invisible labour of centuries and foundations longing for air
There is no way to stop until the arch of flowers and horizons
That signals your triumph

He is the man
The man standing upright above his dreams

HIJA

Tengo tu rostro entre las manos
Oh aire dulce retrato de aire
Anillo del mundo y del pasado
Tu rostro de silencio
Rostro de lámpara tierna
Con qué facilidad te formas en mis ojos
Cómo vuelves alegrando la negrura

Miseria del recuerdo
En el umbral del frío la selva se hace sueño
Se desprenden las hojas
Se mueren las miradas gota a gota

DAUGHTER

I hold your face in my hands
Oh sweet air portrait of air
Arena of the world and of the past
Your silent face
Face like a delicate lamp
How easily you take shape in my eyes
How your return brings light to the darkness

The misery of memory
At the threshold of the cold the forest turns into a dream
Leaves are shed
Attention dies drop by drop

VOZ PREFERIDA

Aquellos cielos derramados entre palomas y montañas
Aquella tierra que llenaba el mundo
Con sus voces marinas y sus ansias
De razas desbordadas y capitanes furibundos
Esa enorme vertiente o corazón inagotable

Ahora al sacudir sus nuevos sueños
Vuelve a tomar su marcha desde el sitio
En donde la epopeya se quedó dormida de cansancio
Entre caballos rodando por la muerte
Entre la altiva historia con el mismo gesto de sol con que saliera

FAVOURITE VOICE

Those skies squandered between doves and mountains
That land which filled the world
With its marine voices and their longings
For kindred larger than life and angry captains
That enormous slope or inexhaustible heart

Now as it shakes off its new dreams
It returns ready to set off from the place
Where the epic fell asleep from exhaustion
While horses were tumbling to their deaths
While the proud story makes the same sunny gesture as when it emerged

LA VIDA ES SUEÑO

Los ojos andan de día en día
Las princesas pasan de rama en rama
Como la sangre de los enanos
Que cae igual que todas sobre las hojas
Cuando llega su hora de noche en noche

Las hojas muertas quieren hablar
Son gemelas de su voz dolorida
Son la sangre de las princesas
Y los ojos de rama en rama
Que caen igual que los astros viejos
Con las alas rotas como corbatas

La sangre cae de rama en rama
De ojo en ojo y de voz en voz
La sangre cae como las corbatas
No puede huir saltando como los enanos
Cuando las princesas pasan
Hacia sus astros doloridos
Como las alas de las hojas
Como los ojos de las olas
Como las hojas de los ojos
Como las olas de las alas

Las horas caen de minuto en minuto
Como la sangre
Que quiere hablar

LIFE IS A DREAM

Eyes wander from day to day
Princesses cross from branch to branch
Like the blood of dwarves
Which falls on leaves just as everyone else's does
Night after night when their time comes

The dead leaves want to speak
They are twins with aching voices
They are the blood of princesses
And the eyes going from branch to branch
Which fall just as old stars do
With broken wings like neckties

Blood falls from branch to branch
From eye to eye and from voice to voice
Blood falls just as neckties do
It cannot flee leaping like a dwarf
When princesses cross over
Towards their aching stars
Like the wings of leaves
Like the eyes of waves
Like the leaves of eyes
Like the waves of wings

The hours fall from moment to moment
Like blood
Wanting to speak

AIRE DE ALBA

Mi alma está sobre el mar y silba un sueño
Decid a los pastores que el viento prepare su caballo
Y saluda al partir en el orgullo de su infancia
Yo amo una mujer de orgullo y sueño
Desembarcando de su fondo silenciosa
Sabed pastores que debéis cuidarme
Y cuidar sus sueños y cuidar sus cantos
Y la fiesta de las olas
Como alegría de su orgullo y su belleza

Ah cielo azul para la reina al viento
Ah rebaño de cabras y cabellos blancos
Labios de elogios y cabellos rubios
Animales perdidos en sus ojos
Hablad a la osamenta que se peina
En el país del fondo hasta el fin de los siglos

Túnica y cetro
Amplificación de los recuerdos
Ruido de insectos y caminos
Hablar de la comarca como corre el océano
Ah el viento
El viento se detiene para la reina que sale de su cielo

DAWN AIR

My soul is above the sea and whistles a dream
Tell the shepherds the wind is preparing its horse
As it leaves it waves with childish pride
I love a woman proud and dreamlike
Putting ashore from her silent depths
Shepherds you know you should look after me
And look after her dreams and look after her songs
And the celebration of the waves
As if from joy in her pride and her beauty

Ah a blue sky for the queen in the wind
Ah a herd of goats and white hair
Acclaimed lips and blond hair
Stray animals in her eyes
You must speak to the skeleton combing its hair
In the land of the deep until the end of ages

Tunic and sceptre
Memories amplified
Noise of insects and roads
Speaking of the region as the ocean flows
Ah the wind
The wind stops for the queen emerging from its sky

LA POESÍA ES
UN ATENTADO CELESTE

Yo estoy ausente pero en el fondo de este ausencia
Hay la espera de mí mismo
Y esta espera es otro modo de presencia
La espera de mi retorno
Yo estoy en otros objetos
Ando en viaje dando un poco de mi vida
A ciertos árboles y a ciertas piedras
Que me han esperado muchos años

Se cansaron de esperarme y se sentaron

Yo no estoy y estoy
Estoy ausente y estoy presente en estado do espera
Ellos querrían mi lenguaje para expresarse
Y yo querría el de ellos para expresarlos
He aquí el equívoco el atroz equívoco

Angustioso lamentable
Me voy adentrando en estas plantas
Voy dejando mis ropas
Se me van cayendo las carnes
Y mi esqueleto se va revistiendo de corteza

Me estoy haciendo árbol Cuántas veces me he ido convirtiendo en
        otras cosas
Es doloroso y lleno de ternura

Podría dar un grito pero se espantaría la transubstanciación
Hay que guardar silencio Esperar en silencio

POETRY IS
A CELESTIAL ASSAULT

I am absent but at the core of this absence
There is an expectation of myself
And this expectation is another type of presence
The expectation of my return
I am there in other objects
I am on a journey giving a little of my life
To some trees and some stones
That have awaited me these many years

They tired of waiting for me and sat down

I am not here and I am
I am absent and I am present on standby
They would like to have my language to express themselves
And I would like to have theirs to express them
Here is the misunderstanding the appalling misunderstanding

Lamentable anxiety
I am going deep inside these plants
I am leaving my clothes behind
My flesh is falling off me
And my skeleton is becoming clad with bark

I am turning into a tree How often have I been transformed into other
    things
It is painful and full of tenderness

I could shout out loud but this would scare off the transubstantiation
Silence must be maintained Wait in silence

LA NOCHE MOMENTÁNEA

Sur le pont d'Avignon
On ne danse plus en rond
Ya no se baila sobre el puente de Avignon Francia
Ni se baila ni se canta en ninguna de tus plazas
Todo es tristeza ahora
Una altiva tristeza que rumia en los adentros
Y prepara el día de los volcanes vengadores

Árbol del sacrificio
Esperando la voz de tus clarines

Para saltar al medio de la hoguera
Y levantar tu nombre

A ese zenit de espejos triunfadores
A ese alto sitio tuyo Francia ese alto sitio
Otorgado por los siglos

Bajel del mundo prepara tu velamen
Este viento contrario que te azota y detiene tu marcha
Ha de cambiarse en viento favorable
Ha de empujarte otra vez en tus rutas ilustres
Entonces los que no hemos aceptado tu derrota
Cantaremos el canto inmenso que levanta los astros
Y aquellos que te entregaron maniatada
Tendrán sólo el suicidio o el fondo de los mares
Que aún es demasiado honor para tanta miseria

Árbol del sacrificio
Henos aquí los que te amamos a tu sombra
Gota a gota la muerte la perfidia
El dolor cae sobre nuestras cabezas
Henos aquí velando tu horrible pesadilla

THE FLEETING NIGHT

Sur le pont d'Avignon
On ne danse plus en rond
No more dancing on the bridge in Avignon France
No dancing or singing in any of your squares
Nothing but sadness now
A haughty sadness that broods inside
And prepares for the day of avenging volcanoes

Tree of sacrifice
Awaiting the sound of your trumpets

To jump right into the pyre
And raise your name

To that zenith of triumphant mirrors
To that high place of yours France that high place
Bestowed by the ages

Vessel of the world prepare your sails
This adverse wind that lashes you and halts your progress
Must be turned into a favourable wind
Must drive you on again on your illustrious path
Then those of us who have not accepted your defeat
Will sing the great song that raises the stars
And those who brought you in manacles
Will have only suicide or the bottom of the sea
Which is still too great an honour for so much misery

Tree of sacrifice
Here we are who love you in your shadows
Drop by drop death treachery
Pain falls on our heads
Here we are maintaining a vigil during your terrible nightmare

Atardece sobre la tierra
Tus águilas atadas sollozan recordando otros días
Recontando epopeyas que rebasan tus campos
Enumerando glorias que no caben en tus límites
Ni sobre los dedos de cuarenta millones de hijos

Sangre de hombres
Esperanza de hombres que construyen destinos
Oh plena de anhelos milenarios
Oh profunda raíz de las edades y vísceras del tiempo

Árbol del sacrificio
Yo canto todo aquello que ha tenido grandeza
Los barcos de aventura entre el misterio
Buscando olas bravías
Los audaces de ojos afiebrados
En la maraña de las selvas o de ideas osadas
Agrandando la vida el pensamiento
Creando tierras y muriendo de sed

El despertar de razas como enormes incendios
El pasado que se proyecta a un gran futuro
Mas no la traición y sus hojas podridas

Silbemos aquí contra las rocas descompuestas
Frente a las ansias torpes y el heroísmo hueco

Árbol del sacrificio
Aquí bajo tu sombra mi corazón me cuenta
Las historias perdidas en los años del mundo
Me habla de las leyes obscuras
Me enseña la lección de la esperanza
He visto Francia
He visto y estoy viendo el rostro de los siglos
Los buscadores incansables
Los árboles que admiran las insignes empresas
El pájaro que endulza al prisionero detrás de los barrotes

Sunset over the earth
Your tethered eagles sob recalling other days
Recounting epics that outgrow your lands
Listing glories that do not fit within your boundaries
Not even on the fingers of forty million children

Blood of men
Hopes of men who build destinies
Oh full of ancient yearnings
Oh deep-rooted ages and the viscera of time

Tree of sacrifice
I sing of all that has possessed greatness
Explorers' boats amidst the mystery
Seeking ferocious waves
Bold ones with feverish eyes
In forest thickets or in daring ideas
Amplifying life thoughts
Creating land and dying of thirst

The awakening of the race like a huge blaze
The past projected into a great future
But not treachery and its decaying leaves

Let us whistle here against the broken rocks
As against clumsy cravings and hollow heroism

Tree of sacrifice
Here in your shade my heart tells me
Stories lost through the world's years
It speaks to me of obscure laws
Teaches me the lesson of hope
I have seen France
I have seen and I am seeing the face of the centuries
The tireless seekers
The trees that admire illustrious enterprises
The bird that makes life bearable for the prisoner behind bars

Los castillos con un alma que hila en una rueca
Los grandes alaridos que derrumben murallas
Las montañas emocionadas por la bravura y el esfuerzo
El caballo llorando al caballero muerto

Yo te he visto Francia
Semejante a primer arco iris del mundo
Yo te he visto semejante a un astro derramando ensueños
Yo te he visto orgullosa y parecida al huracán
Yo te he visto amada mía
Dulce como una fruta preparada por los tiempos
Para el sabor universal
Te he visto cuando abrías el alba
Y te abrías al designio
Francia
Se asusta el hombre cuando tú enmudeces

En este juego de la Historia
En este juego subterráneo y tremendo
En donde los impulsos se forman y deforman
En donde les fuerzas se deshacen
Y buscan un equilibrio nuevo
En este juego de la Historia fatal y triunfadora
Donde el barco no puede elegir sus olas
Hoy te ha tocado la noche
(Que sea breve es mi deseo)
Pronto que vuelva pronto *le temps de cerises*
Oh bergère bergère rentre tes noirs moutons

Francia en esos campos trágicos
Donde los hombres caen como la noche
Te dieron un brebaje de hierbas venenosas
Ahora estás soñando que una hiena devora tus entrañas
Una hada maligna te ha dormido
En un lecho de sangre
Pero no pudo cambiarte en monstruo repugnante
El hechizo no será perdurable

Castles with souls spinning round in a wheel
Great screams bringing down walls
Mountains excited by bravery and effort
A horse mourning the dead knight

I have seen you France
Just like the world's first rainbow
I have seen you looking like a star spilling daydreams
I have seen you proud and resembling a hurricane
I have seen you my beloved
Sweet as a fruit prepared by time
For universal taste
I have seen you when you opened the dawn
And you were open to the plan
France
It frightens mankind when you stay silent

In this game of History
In this tremendous subterranean game
Where momentum forms and deforms
Where forces unravel
And seek a new equilibrium
In this fatal and triumphant game of History
Where the boat may not choose its waves
Today you have been touched by night
(May it be brief is my sole wish)
Soon may you come back soon *le temps de cerises*
Oh bergère bergère rentre tes noirs moutons

France on those tragic fields
Where men fall like night
They gave you a potion of poisonous herbs
Now you are dreaming that a hyena devours your guts
An evil witch has put you to sleep
In a bed of blood
But she could not change you into a repulsive monster
The spell will not endure

Ya viene el caballero a despertarte
Escucha el paso de los tuyos
Que se acercar corriendo entre fantasmas
Por los bosques donde otros se perdieron

Árbol del sacrificio
Gritemos a los vientos que hay que enjugar las lágrimas
Y preparar las armas de la aurora
Francia mi dulce Francia
Con su vieja cordura y sus altos delirios
Aún hay muchos que creemos en ti
Oh necesaria a la tierra como la primavera
Tú eres la puerta de los sueños
Eres la madre humana comprensiva y sonriente
La primera mirada a la primera estrella
La última mirada a la postrera
El primer aplauso el último saludo
Flor de profecías y relámpagos
Eres la puerta por donde entra el corazón al mundo

Henos aquí a tu sombra
Contemplando tu noche momentánea
Oh tristeza oh pájaro sin canto
Cuánto tiempo ha de durar nuestra desgracia
(Que sea breve es mi deseo)

Árbol del sacrificio
Aquí bajo tu sombra
He de verte volver del fondo de la noche
Trayendo tus recuerdos encendidos de nuevo
Tus grandes ojos abiertos a los cielos
Trayendo tu estrella como un libro de luz entre las manos
Al seguir tu camino dejando atrás las sombras
Oirás una voz nueva que cae del espacio
Y te llena de impulsos porque tiene algo tuyo

The knight is coming to wake you
Listen for the footsteps of your loved ones
As they approach running amongst phantoms
Through the woods where others were lost

Tree of sacrifice
Let us shout to the winds that the tears must be wiped away
And prepare the weapons of dawn
France my sweet France
With her old sanity and her lofty delusions
There are still many who believe in you
Oh needed by the earth as much as Spring
You are the door to dreams
You are the human mother with an understanding smile
The first look at the first star
The final look at the last one
The first applause the final greeting
Flower of prophecies and lightning bolts
You are the door through which our hearts enter the world

Here we are in your shadow
Contemplating your fleeting night
Oh sadness oh bird with no song
How long must our misfortune last
(May it be brief is my sole wish)

Tree of sacrifice
Here under your shadow
I have to see you return from the depths of night
Bringing your glowing memories once again
Your great eyes open to the heavens
Bringing your star like a book of light between your hands
As you go your way leaving the shadow behind
You will hear a new voice falling from space
And it urges you on because it has something of yours

Francia
Despertemos de esta larga pesadilla
Hay que romper la telaraña que te envuelve
Encender otra vez la antorcha del destino
Entre tanto agonizante y tanta niebla
Francia bailemos la *Carmagnole*

France
Let us awake from this long nightmare
The spider's web that surrounds you must be broken
Light the torch of destiny again
In the midst of so much dying and so much fog
France let us dance the *Carmagnole*

EL HIJO CANTA
A LA MADRE DOLOROSA

Ese inmenso sollozo de tu pecho FRANCIA es para los hombres
Esa herida que sangra a cielo perdido es para la vida
Ellos no comprendieron la lección de tu alma
Acaso era demasiado grande tu palabra
Y nadie pudo descifrarla
Este inmenso dolor que te curva es para el mundo
Mas he aquí lo que debe consolarte
Cuando tú sufres la tierra siente tu sufrimiento
Cuando tú lloras tus lágrimas ruedan por el rostro de la Historia
Por el rostro de todo ser que se ilumina por dentro
Y que tiene conocimiento de su propia especie
Esta es tu grandeza y tus raíces en la raíz humana

Sólo tú puedes soportar el peso del desastre
Tal es tu fuerza tal es el fuego de tu huella entre los hombres
Oh FRANCIA no digas nunca cuánto has sufrido
Ninguna entraña podría soportarlo

Oh bien amada Oh grito de sangre
Te siento palpitar en mi garganta
Paloma herida en sus montañas
Oh princesa sorprendida en la emboscada
Habla de nuevo de nuevo deja oír tu voz
La Tierra se pierde entre los astros cuando te impiden guiar su marcha
Oh flor perfecta en medio de tantas cosas horribles
Siempre la primera en nuestra esperanza
FRANCIA a través de todas nuestras lágrimas
Relámpago y trueno en el fondo de todo pecho
Yo te digo al oído las palabras de mi alma
Porque ella te debe su mitad más profunda
Te bendigo en tu cólera te canto en tu angustia

THE CHILD SINGS
TO OUR LADY OF SORROWS

That huge sob from your breast FRANCE is for mankind
That wound which bleeds into the lost sky is for life
They did not understand the lessons from your soul
Perhaps your words were too great
And no one could decipher them
This enormous pain that makes you buckle is for the world
But here is something that should comfort you
When you suffer the earth feels your suffering
When you weep your tears roll down the face of History
Down the face of every being with inner light
And that has any knowledge of its own species
This is your greatness and your roots lie in the human race

Only you can bear the weight of the disaster
Such is your strength such is the fire of your impact on mankind
Oh FRANCE never say how much you've suffered
No soul could bear it

Oh well beloved Oh cry for blood
I feel you throbbing in my throat
Dove wounded in the mountains
Oh princess caught in an ambush
Speak again once again let your voice be heard
The Earth is lost amongst the stars when you are prevented from leading
      the way
Oh perfect flower in the midst of so many horrible things
Always first amongst our hopes
FRANCE through all our tears
Thunder and lightning in the depths of every breast
I tell you to your face the words from my soul
Because it owes you her most profound part
I bless you in your anger I sing to you in your despair

Alba cubierta do un sudario donde yace el nacimiento de un águila
La substancia da los leones futuros

Madre de las grandes épocas y de las edades supremas
Sembradora de ideas sobre las más altas cumbres
Que tu pesar no vele tus ojos donde cada uno descubre su belleza
Tu día ce aproxima y tú debes preparar tu estrella
Nosotros tenemos siempre confianza en ti
El corazón del mundo ruge de libertad
Está siempre en tu pecho

Oh FRANCIA tú eres aún nuestro mejor impulso
Eres siempre la tierra bajo nuestros pies
Eres siempre el cielo sobre nuestra cabeza
Eres siempre el trigo de nuestro pan
Siempre la leche de las ovejas vagando en nuestros sueños
Todo hombre que tiene el orgullo y el respeto de su alma
Sabe que tú eras la misma aún engrandecida por el dolor

Despiértate princesa de esta larga pesadilla
El ogro que vertió el veneno tiene sus horas contadas
Y conoce ya el sitio de su tumba
Levántate aún eres nuestra luz
Te esperamos al borde de la selva encantada
Para seguir contigo nuevos caminos

Tú eres siempre la más fraternal amiga
La estación de las hojas el arco iris cantante
Eres siempre el signo del Destino

Dawn covered by a shroud where the birth of an eagle takes place
The essence of future lions

Mother of the greatest ages and of supreme ages
Sower of ideas on the highest summits
May your sorrow not veil your eyes where each discovers their beauty
Your day is near and you must prepare your star
We always have confidence in you
The heart of the world roars with freedom
It is always in your breast

Oh FRANCE you are still our finest impulse
You are always the earth beneath our feet
You are always the sky above our heads
You are always the wheat for our bread
Always the milk from sheep roaming in our dreams
Every man who is proud and respects his own soul
Knows you were the same although swollen with sorrow

Awake princess from this long nightmare
The ogre who poured the poison has his days numbered
And already knows the site of his grave
Arise you are still our light
We await you at the edge of the enchanted forest
To follow new paths by your side

You are always the most fraternal friend
The leafy season the singing rainbow
You are always the sign of Destiny

UNA TARDE
DESPUÉS DEL RHIN

Qué pequeño es el mundo
Cuán grande eres corazón
Mirado desde aquí
En medio del torbellino de esta guerra
Qué pequeños se ven los hombres
Qué triste el cielo y el mar y las montañas
Y cuán desierta el alma humana
Amargura y dolor
Desamparados seres que caminan
Porque hay que caminar
Sin rumbo sin destino
Equivocando el signo o perdiendo su estrella
Inmensa marcha tras quimeras vacías
Agitación inútil Hay que llorar
Mas los árboles ríen de nosotros

Niños pequeños con ojos que se agrandan
Al mirarnos pasar
¿Cómo no lloran? ¿O no saben llorar?
¿De qué se trata? ¿Comprendéis algo?
¡Qué angustia! ¡Qué inmensa soledad!
¿En dónde estáis recuerdos de mi vida?
¿Tengo acaso recuerdos?
Las lágrimas tragadas
Cuánto más duras son que aquellas otras
Que aman los arroyos
¿Quién ha sembrado tanto mal?
¿Quién despertó las selvas de serpientes?

Oh estrella mía
Qué pretendes de mí?

ONE EVENING BEYOND THE RHINE

How small the world is
How great you are heart
Seen from here
Amidst the whirlwind of this war
How small men look
How sad the sky and the sea and the mountains
And how deserted the human soul
Bitterness and pain
Forsaken beings who walk
Because they have to walk
With no direction no destination
Misunderstanding the signs or losing their star
Great pursuit of empty chimeras
Useless agitation One can only weep
But the trees laugh at us

Young children whose eyes widen
As they watch us pass
How come they don't cry? Or don't they know how?
What's this about? Do you understand anything?
What anguish! What immense loneliness!
Where are you memories of my life?
Do I have any memories?
Tears swallowed
How much harder they are than those others
That love riverbeds
Who has sowed so much evil?
Who woke the snakes in the jungle?

Oh my star
What do you want from me?

Hacia dónde me llevas?
¿Por qué me traes a la sangre?
¿No ves que todo se hizo herida en mi garganta?

Oh ceguera del mundo
Destruye de una vez la grandeza que odias
Y que no se hable más y no se cante y no se ría

Un siglo de silencio para enterrar los muertos

Where are you taking me?
Why do you make me bleed?
Can you not see that everything gets injured in my throat?

Oh blindness of the world
Destroy at once the greatness that you hate
And do not talk anymore and do not sing and do not laugh

A century of silence to bury the dead

[DÍAS Y NOCHES TE HE BUSCADO]

Días y noches te he buscado
Sin encontrar el sitio en donde cantas
Te he buscado por el tiempo arriba y por el río abajo
Te has perdido entre las lágrimas

Noches y noches te he buscado
Sin encontrar el sitio en donde lloras
Porque yo sé que estás llorando
Me basta con mirarme en un espejo
Para saber que estás llorando y me has llorado

Sólo tú salvas el llanto
Y de mendigo obscuro lo haces rey coronado por tu mano

[DAYS AND NIGHTS
I HAVE SEARCHED FOR YOU]

Days and nights I have searched for you
Without finding the place where you sing
I have searched for you up time and down river
You are lost amidst your tears

Night after night I have searched for you
Without finding the place where you weep
Because I know you are weeping
It is enough for me to regard myself in the mirror
To know that you are weeping and you have wept for me

You alone save your tears
And an obscure beggar is crowned king by your own hand

[QUIERO DESAPARECER
Y NO MORIR]

Quiero desaparecer y no morir
Quiero no ser y perdurar
Y saber que perduro
Llamo a las puertas de la muerte
Y me retiro
Llamo a la vida y huyo avergonzado
Quiero ser toda mi alma y no lo puedo
Quiero todo mi cuerpo y no lo logro

[I WANT TO DISAPPEAR AND NOT TO DIE]

I want to disappear and not to die
I want not to exist and to endure
And to know that I will endure
I knock on death's door
And I withdraw
I call to life and I flee in shame
I want to be all my soul but can not
I want all my body but I do not manage it

[LA NOCHE VIENE
A ESPERARSE EN MÍ]

La noche viene a esperarse en mí
Los astros inauguran sus abismos
Para vivir fuera de la verde presencia
Para tener su encuentro en ojos olvidados
Aunque seguros de sus lluvias
Como un espacio que va a hacerse nieve

La noche me ha elegido para sí misma
Me dice al oído cosas de su agua
Y que somos capaces de cualquier crimen
Como de la mayor bondad y grandes sacrificios

[NIGHT COMES AND PUTS ITS HOPES IN ME]

Night comes and puts its hopes in me
The stars unveil their chasms
So they can live beyond the green presence
So they can rendezvous in forgotten eyes
Although safe from their rains
Like a place where snow is about to fall

Night has chosen me for itself
It whispers in my ear something about its waters
And that we are capable of any crime whatsoever
As well as of the greatest goodness and grand sacrifices

MONUMENTO AL MAR

Paz sobre la constelación cantante de las aguas
Entrechocadas como los hombros de la multitud
Paz en el mar a las olas de buena voluntad
Paz sobre la lápida de los naufragios
Paz sobre los tambores del orgullo y las pupilas tenebrosas
Y si yo soy el traductor de las olas
Paz también sobre mí

He aquí el molde lleno de trizaduras del destino
El molde de la venganza
Con sus frases iracundas despegándose de los labios
He aquí el molde lleno de gracia
Cuando eres dulce y estás allí hipnotizado por las estrellas
He aquí la muerte inagotable desde el principio del mundo
Porque un día nadie se paseará por el tiempo
Nadie a lo largo del tiempo empedrado de planetas difuntos

Este es el mar
El mar con sus olas propias
Con sus propios sentidos
El mar tratando de romper sus cadenas
Queriendo imitar la eternidad
Queriendo ser pulmón o neblina de pájaros en pena
O el jardín de los astros que pesan en el cielo
Sobre las tinieblas que arrastramos
O que acaso nos arrastran
Cuando vuelan de repente todas las palomas de la luna
Y se hace más obscuro que las encrucijadas de la muerte

El mar entra en la carroza de la noche
Y se aleja hacia el misterio de sus parajes profundos
Se oye apenas el ruido de las ruedas
Y el ala de los astros que penan en el cielo

MONUMENT TO THE SEA

Peace be upon the singing constellation of waters
Colliding like shoulders in a crowd
Peace at sea to waves of good will
Peace be upon the tombstones of the shipwrecked
Peace be upon the drums of pride and dark eyes
And if I am translator for the waves
Peace be upon me also

Here is the mould filled with shreds of destiny
The mould of revenge
With furious words spat from its lips
Here is the mould filled with grace
When you are gentle and stand there hypnotized by the stars
Here is death inexhaustible from the beginning of the world
Because one day no-one will stroll though time
No-one throughout the course of time paved with dead planets

This is the sea
The sea with its own waves
With its own meanings
The sea trying to break its chains
Wishing to imitate eternity
Wishing to be a jellyfish or a haze of sorrowful birds
Or the garden with stars weighing down the sky
Above the darkness we drag with us
Or perhaps that is dragging us
When suddenly all the doves on the moon fly off
And it gets darker than the crossroads of death

The sea enters night's carriage
And heads for the mystery of its deepest places
The sound of the wheels can hardly be heard
Nor the line of stars suffering in the sky

Éste es el mar
Saludando allá lejos la eternidad
Saludando a los astros olvidados
Y a las estrellas conocidas

Éste es el mar que se despierta como el llanto de un niño
El mar abriendo los ojos y buscando el sol con sus pequeñas manos
          temblorosas
El mar empujando las olas
Sus olas que barajan los destinos

Levántate y saluda el amor de los hombres

Escucha nuestras risas y también nuestro llanto
Escucha los pasos de millones de esclavos
Escucha la protesta interminable
De esa angustia que se llama hombre
Escucha el dolor milenario de los pechos de carne
Y la esperanza que renace de sus propias cenizas cada día

También nosotros te escuchamos
Rumiando tantos astros atrapados en tus redes
Rumiando eternamente los siglos naufragados
También nosotros te escuchamos
Cuando te revuelcas en tu lecho de dolor
Cuando tus gladiadores se baten entre sí
Cuando tu cólera hace estallar los meridianos
O bien cuando te agitas como un gran mercado en fiesta
O bien cuando maldices a los hombres
O te haces el dormido
Tembloroso en tu gran telaraña esperando la presa

Lloras sin saber por qué lloras
Y nosotros lloramos creyendo saber por qué lloramos
Sufres sufres como sufren los hombres
Que oiga rechinar tus dientes en la noche

This is the sea
Greeting eternity there in the distance
Greeting stars it had forgotten
And stars it recognised

This is the sea which awakens like the crying of a child
The sea opening its eyes and searching for the sun with its trembling
       little hands
The sea pushing waves
Its waves that reshuffle destinies

Stand up and greet the love of mankind

Listen to our laughter and also to our weeping
Listen to the footsteps of millions of slaves
Listen to the never-ending protest
Of that anxiety called mankind
Listen to the age-old sorrow in flesh-covered breasts
And to the hope reborn from its own ashes every day

Also we listen to you
Pondering so many stars caught in your nets
Pondering the foundered centuries for evermore
Also we listen to you
When you toss and turn on your bed of sorrow
When your gladiators fight amongst themselves
When your anger makes the meridians erupt
Or even when you become stirred up like a great festival market
Or even when you curse mankind
Or you play dead
Trembling in your great web awaiting your prey

You weep without knowing why you weep
And we weep believing we know why we weep
You suffer you suffer as mankind suffers
May I hear your teeth grinding during the night

Y te revuelques en tu lecho
Que el insomnio no te deje calmar tus sufrimientos
Que los niños apedreen tus ventanas
Que te arranquen el pelo
Tose tose revienta en sangre tus pulmones
Que tus resortes enmohezcan
Y te veas pisoteado como césped de tumba

Pero soy vagabundo y tengo miedo que me oigas
Tengo miedo de tus venganzas
Olvida mis maldiciones y cantemos juntos esta noche
Hazte hombre te digo como yo a veces me hago mar
Olvida los presagios funestos
Olvida la explosión de mis praderas
Yo te tiendo las manos como flores
Hagamos las paces te digo
Tú eres el más poderoso
Que yo estreche tus manos en las mías
Y sea la paz entre nosotros

Junto a mi corazón te siento
Cuando oigo el gemir de tus violines
Cuando estás ahí tendido como el llanto de un niño
Cuando estás pensativo frente al cielo
Cuando estás dolorido en tus almohadas
Cuando te siento llorar detrás de mi ventana
Cuando lloramos sin razón como tú lloras

He aquí el mar
El mar donde viene a estrellarse el olor de las ciudades
Con su regazo llena de barcas y peces y otras cosas alegres
Esas barcas que pescan a la orilla del cielo
Esos peces que escuchan cada rayo de luz
Esas algas con sueños seculares
Y ese ola que canta mejor que las otras
He aquí el mar
El mar que se estira y se aferra a sus orillas

And may you toss and turn on your bed
May insomnia permit no relief of your suffering
May children throw stones at your windows
May they pull out your hair
Cough cough may your lungs burst with blood
May your springs get rusty
And may you see yourself trampled like the grass around a grave

But I am a rover and fear you might hear me
I fear your vengeance
Forget my curses and let us sing together tonight
Act like a man I tell you as I at times act like a sea
Forget the dismal omens
Forget the explosion of my pastures
I stretch out my hands to you like flowers
Let us make peace I say to you
You are the stronger
Let me hold your hands in mine
And may there be peace between us

I feel you next to my heart
When I hear the groaning of your violins
When you lie here like a weeping child
When you are thoughtful facing the sky
When you are in pain amongst your pillows
When I hear you weeping behind my window
When we weep for no reason the way you weep

Here is the sea
The sea where the scent of cities comes crashing down
With a lap full of boats and fish and other happy things
Those boats fishing by the shores of the sky
Those fish listening to every ray of light
That seaweed with secular dreams
And that wave which sings better than the others
Here is the sea
The sea that unfolds and clings to its shores

El mar que envuelve les estrellas en sus olas
El mar con su piel martirizada
Y los sobresaltos de sus venas
Con sus días de paz y sus noches de histeria

Y al otro lado qué hay al otro lado
Qué escondes mar al otro lado
El comienzo de la vida largo como una serpiente
O el comienzo de la muerte más honda que tú mismo
Y más alta que todos los montes
Qué hay al otro lado
La milenaria voluntad de hacer una forma y un ritmo
O el torbellino eterno de pétalos tronchados

He ahí el mar
El mar abierto de par en par
He ahí el mar quebrado de repente
Para que el ojo vea el comienzo del mundo
He ahí el mar
De una ola a la otra hay el tiempo de la vida
De sus olas a mis ojos hay la distancia de la muerte

The sea that envelops stars in its waves
The sea with its tormented skin
And sudden jolts in its veins
With its days of peace and its nights of hysteria

And on the other side what is there on the other side
Sea what is that you're hiding on the other side
The beginning of a life as long as a snake
Or the beginning of a death more intense than yourself
And higher than all the mountains
What is there on the other side
The age-old desire to create form and rhythm
Or the eternal whirlwind of pruned petals

Here is the sea
The sea wide open all the way
Here is the sea turned suddenly rough
So the eye can see the beginning of the world
Here is the sea
Between one wave and the next lies the span of life
Between your waves and my eyes lies the distance of death

[PIENSO EN ELLOS
EN LOS MUERTOS]

Pienso en ellos en los muertos
En los que yo vi caer
En los que están grabados en mi alma
En los que aún están cayendo en mis miradas
Vosotros que seguiréis muriendo
Hasta el día en que yo muera

[I THINK OF THEM
I THINK OF THE DEAD]

I think of them I think of the dead
Of those I saw falling
Of those who are carved into my soul
Of those who keep falling before my eyes
You who will go on dying
Until the day when I die

[TIERRA QUE TE ALIMENTAS DE MI TRISTEZA]

Tierra que te alimentas de mi tristeza
Que gozas de beber mi sangre
Y cada herida de mi pecho te enriquece
Eres hermosa como una gran borrasca
¡Cómo te gusta mi soledad!
Eres terrible como una alma grandiosa
Que se defiende sola contra todas las ansias
Te esperaré escondido
En una encrucijada donde menos lo pienses
Y lucharemos cuerpo a cuerpo
Tierra que te alimentas de mi tristeza
Nací con siglos de amargura
Pero vamos a ver quién ríe ahora

[LAND YOU FEED ON MY SADNESS]

Land how you feed on my sadness
How you enjoy drinking my blood
And every wound in my breast enriches you
You are as fine as a great storm
How do you like my loneliness!
You are as terrible as a great soul
That defends itself against all cravings
I will wait for you in hiding
At a crossroads where you will least expect it
And we will fight hand to hand
Land how you feed on my sadness
I was born with centuries of bitterness
But we will see who's laughing now

[ALMA SEDUCIDA POR SU RAZA]

Alma seducida por su raza
Por los vientos lejanos
Por las alturas que humillan las miradas
Por las profundidades que desesperan los ojos
Nunca cambies tu voz
Por una rosa de nácar
Por un miraje de aire
Sin real embrujamiento

[SOUL SEDUCED BY ITS LINEAGE]

Soul seduced by its lineage
By distant winds
By heights that humiliate their observers
By depths that make one's eyes despair
Never change your voice
For a mother-of-pearl rose
For an airy mirage
With no real sorcery

[TE AMO MUJER
DE MI GRAN VIAJE]

Te amo mujer de mi gran viaje
Como el mar ama al agua
Que lo hace existir
Y le da derecho a llamarse mar
Y a reflejar el cielo y la luna y las estrellas

[I LOVE YOU WOMAN FROM MY GREAT JOURNEY]

I love you woman from my great journey
As the sea loves the water
That allows it to exist
And gives it the right to call itself sea
And to reflect the sky and the moon and the stars

[VAGABA POR LAS CALLES DE UNA CIUDAD HELADA]

Vagaba por las calles de una ciudad helada
Con tanta noche encima
Triste como el espacio que queda
Entre un farol y la casa desierta

[I WANDERED THE STREETS OF A FROZEN CITY]

I wandered the streets of a frozen city
With so much night above me
Sad as the space that remains
Between a street lamp and the deserted house

ILUSIONES PERDIDAS

Hoja del árbol caída en infancia
Hoja caída de rodillas
En el centro de su olvido
Dulce juguete de esperanzas y relámpagos
Sangrando la cabeza mal herida
Como las ilusiones ópticas
En su palacio de muerte inolvidable
Constante barco de corazón doliente
Entre naufragio y sombra apresurada

Hoja del nudo caído en árbol caído en infancia
Adonde te arrastran hoja de dulce corazón
Y los excesos del fuego de las águilas visuales
Hojas de las ramas calefaccionables
Detenidas en el aire
Prontas a podredumbre entre sus propios brazos
Como las aguas embrujadas

Hojas de fantasmas sorprendidos
Hojas de pájaros escritos
Cada una tiene su caballo y su paloma
Cada una tiene su horizonte a todo precio
Y no hay árbol ni velamen para su amargura

Hojas del árbol caídas
En la cabeza del poeta
En su deseo de llorar porque no llega nunca
Eso que espera al fin de cada verso
Eso que aguarda detrás de toda sombra

LOST ILLUSIONS

Leaf fallen from the tree in childhood
Leaf fallen to its knees
In the midst of its oblivion
Sweet plaything of hope and lightning
The badly wounded head bleeding
Like optical illusions
In its palace of unforgettable death
Constant boat with an aching heart
Between shipwreck and driven shadows

Leaf from the fallen knot in a tree fallen in childhood
Where are they hauling you sweet-hearted leaf
And the abuses of fire by the eagles we see
Leaves from heated branches
Suspended in the air
Ready to rot in their own arms
Like haunted waters

Leaves from surprised phantoms
Leaves from written birds
Each one has its own horse and its own dove
Each one has its own horizon whatever the price
And there is neither tree nor candle for its bitterness

Leaves fallen from the tree
In the poet's head
In his desire to weep because
What is waiting at the end of every verse
What lies behind every shadow
Never comes

[UNA NOCHE DE CAMPOS PROFUNDOS]

Una noche de campos profundos
Una noche de frases como miradas de muerto
Como cielo y cabellera sobre nidos viejos
Una noche de tierra y música perdida
Sientes una flor interna que se aleja
Avergonzado de la vida y sus esperas

[A NIGHT
OF DENSE FIELDS]

A night of dense fields
A night of words like the gaze of the dead
Like sky and hair over old nests
A night of earth and lost music
You sense an inner flower that withdraws
Ashamed of life and its hopes

EXTERIOR

Árboles cerrados a toda aventura
Arboles cerrados a la lámpara triste
Los faros de piel viva sobre las rosas del adiós
La imagen guardada para un viaje
Alma mía ésta es la leyenda de los años
Que detesta la casa estable y el astro de hierros fríos

Otros buscan un rey leproso que adorar
Una gloria de cúpulas el mármol de una noche larga
Vagar sobre truenos de aire sucio
Ninguno declina sus resortes
Y saluda al mundo y sus montañas

He creado carne y llanto
He creado luz y abismo
Me he sentado a cantar
Sobre la cumbre mojada de ternuras y violencias
En donde empieza el aire de la eternidad

Ningún aliento hace subir el día
Ninguna mano hace saltar la noche
Los astros de los grandes adivinos
Apenas pueden secar el canto de las aguas
Por el camino de los signos altivos
Se va la voluntad hacia la muerte
Se van los dioses a la cifra exacta
Por el camino de los monstruos
Se van los ruidos de la muerte
Por el camino de les hojas
Se van los ojos de la muerte
Por el camino de la tarde
Se va la muerte de la impaciencia
Y un ruido de esqueleto gira al fondo del río

OUTSIDE

Trees closed to all adventure
Trees closed to the sad lantern
Beacons of living skin over the roses of farewell
The image saved for a journey
My soul this is the legend of the ages
That despises the secure house and the star of cold iron

Others seek a leper king to worship
A glory of domes the marble of a long night
Wandering over thunderstorms of dusty air
No one resists their influence
Or greets the world and its mountains

I have created flesh and tears
I have created light and chasms
I have sat down to sing
On the summit damp with tenderness and violence
Where the air of eternity begins

No breath makes the day rise
No hand makes the night jump
The stars of the great soothsayers
Can scarcely dry the singing waters
On the path of lofty signs
Free will departs to its death
The gods depart with the exact code
On the path of monsters
The sounds of death depart
On the leafy path
The eyes of death depart
On the evening path
The death of impatience departs
And the sound of a skeleton swirls at the bottom of the river

[AHORA QUE MIS OJOS VUELAN]

Ahora que mis ojos vuelan entre planetas ajenos
Como una botella en alta mar
O en un cielo de todos colores
Sin una sola casa donde entrar en la tarde
Ahora que mis manos escaparon del fuego
En una barca tan rápida como el ocaso
Y casi más que la muerte huyendo del caballo que quiere morderla

Ahora hace frío por el odio que nos tienen las montañas
Hace frío porque se han dicho palabras tristes
Se ha dicho barca ocaso y ojos
Que son una misma cosa

Yo amo el viento que viene de los astros
Envolviendo los rayos cósmicos tan buscados por los hombres
Mientras ellos sólo se interesan por ciertas hierbas
De sabor delicado y olor penetrante
Tan penetrante como ellos mismos
Yo amo los ojos de grandes alas
Y amo el ocaso tan rápido como une barca
Y las manos y la montaña que se deja acariciar
Y una roca llena de amor que desafía al mar
Y un mar que desafía todas las estrellas
Amo el árbol viejo que tiene muchos niños
Un paisaje inmortal mirando nacer sus flores
Un río de cabellos blancos que aun salta entre las piedras
Unos ojos y unas manos salvadas del incendio
Un corazón que late
Como un sapo casi aplastado por una carreta
Y una selva de todos colores
Sin ningún sentido del bien y del mal
Una selva encima de la selva
Para la ternura de los pájaros perdidos
Allá tan lejos de su país natal

[NOW THAT MY EYES FLY]

Now that my eyes fly amongst distant planets
Like a bottle on the high seas
Or in a sky of every colour
Without a single house to enter in the afternoon
Now that my hands escaped the fire
In a boat as swift as the sunset
And almost more than death fleeing from the horse trying to bite it

Now it is cold because of the hatred the mountains have for us
It is cold because sad words have been uttered
The words boat sunset and eyes have been uttered
And are all one and the same

I love the wind winding from the stars
Shrouding the cosmic rays so sought after by mankind
While they are really only interested in a few herbs
With a delicate taste and penetrating smell
As penetrating as themselves
I love the eyes with great wings
And I love the sunset swift as a boat
And the hands and the mountain that lets itself be stroked
And a rock full of love that defies the sea
And a sea that defies all the stars
I love the old tree that has many children
An immortal landscape watching the birth of its flowers
A river of white hair that still jumps between stones
A few eyes a few hands saved from the fire
A heart that beats
Like a toad almost flattened by a cart
And a forest of all colours
With no sense of good or evil
A forest above the forest
For the tenderness of lost birds
So far away there from its native land

EDAD NEGRA

La muerte atravesada de truenos vivos
Atravesada de fríos humanos
La muerte de sobra llamando tierra por la tierra
Y de subida en los rostros amargos
La marea apresurada
Sobre los ojos y las piedras
Cómo decir al mundo si es necesario tanto hielo
Si exige el tiempo tal suplicio
Para futuras voces nuevas

¿En dónde estás flor de las tumbas
Si todo es tumba en el reino infinito?
Sólo se oye la lengua del sepulcro
Llamando a grandes gritos
Las campanas secretas
En su misterio de memorias a la deriva
Semejantes al temblor eterno
Que se separa de les astros

No hay sacrificio demasiado grande
Para la noche que se aleje
Para encontrar una belleza escondida en el fuego

Perderlo todo
Perder los ojos y los brazos
Perder la voz el corazón y sus monstruos delicados
Perder la vida y sus luces internas
Perder hasta la muerte
Perderse entero sin un lamento
Ser sangre y soledad
Ser maldición y bendición de horrores
Tristeza de planeta sin olor de agua
Pasar de ángel a fantasma geológico

DARK AGE

Death permeated by live thunder
Permeated by human chills
Death in abundance summoning earth through the earth
And increasingly so on bitter faces
The rushing tide
Above the eyes and the pebbles
How to tell the world if so much ice is needed
If time demands such suffering
For future new voices

Where are you graveyard flowers
If everything is a grave in the infinite realm?
Only speech from the grave can be heard
Called out with loud cries
The secret bells
Adrift in their mysterious memories
Resembling the eternal quake
That breaks away from the stars

No sacrifice is too great
For the departing night
To find something beautiful hidden in the fire

Losing all of it
Losing eyes and arms
Losing voice heart and their delicate beasts
Losing life and its internal lights
Losing until death
Losing oneself completely with no complaint
Being blood and solitude
Being malediction and benediction of horrors
Sadness of a planet without the smell of water
Going from angel to geological phantom

Y sonreír al sueño que se acerca
Y tanto exige para ser monumento al calor de las manos

Penan los astros como sombres de lobos muertos
En donde está esa región tan prometida y tan buscada
Penan las selvas como venganzas no cumplidas
Con sus vientos amontonados por el suelo
Y el crujir de sus muebles
Mientras el tiempo forja sus quimeras
Debo llorar al hombre y al amigo
La tempestad lo arroja a otras comarcas
Más lejos de lo que él pensaba

Así dirá la Historia
Se debatía entre el furor y la esperanza
Corrían a encender montañas
Y se quemaban en la hoguera
Empujaban ciudades y llanuras
Flanqueaban ríos y mares con la cabeza ensangrentada
Avanzaban en medio de la sombra espía
Caían desplomados como pájaros ilusos
Sus mujeres ardían y clamaban como relámpagos
Los caballos chocaban miembros en el fango
Carros de hierro aviones triturados
Tendidos en el mismo sueño
Guárdate niño de seguir tal ruta

And smiling at the approaching dream
And it demands so much to be a monument in the warmth of one's hands

The stars manifest like the shadows of dead wolves
Where is that region so promised so sought after
The forests manifest like unfulfilled vengeance
With their winds piled on the ground
And the creaking of their furniture
As time forges its chimeras
I have to mourn man and friend
The storm hurls him into other regions
Further away than he expected

That is how History will tell it
There was a debate between rage and hope
They ran to set mountains alight
And were burned at the stake
They pushed cities and plains
Flanked rivers and seas with bloodied heads
Advanced amidst the spying shadows
Fell from the sky like gullible birds
Their women burned and cried out like lightning
Horses clashed limbs in the mud
Iron carts crushed aeroplanes
Laid out in the same dream
Beware child of following such a path

MADRE

Oh sangre mía
Qué has hecho
Cómo es posible que te fueras
Sin importarte las distancias
Sin pensar en el tiempo
Oh sangre mía
Es inútil tu ausencia
Puesto que estás en mis adentros
Puesto que eres la esencia de mi vida
Oh sangre mía
Una lágrima viene rodando
Me estás llorando
Porque yo soy el muerto que quedó en el camino

Dulce profundidad de mis arterias
Oh sangre mía
Tan inútil tu ausencia
Flor-paloma en dónde estás ahora
Con la energía de tus alas
Y la ternura de tu alma

MOTHER

O blood of mine
What have you done?
How is it possible that you left
As if distance were of no concern to you
Without any thought for time
O my blood
Your absence is pointless
Since you are in my heart
Since you are the essence of my life
O blood of mine
A tear comes rolling down
You are mourning me
Because I am the dead man who got in the way

Sweet depths of my arteries
O blood of mine
Your absence so futile
Flower-dove where you are now
With the energy of your wings
And the tenderness of your soul

[LOS LABIOS PRETENDEN ALEJARSE DE LA BOCA]

Los labios pretenden alejarse de la boca
Correr por otros lados
Con presunciones de infinito
Los latidos pretenden abandonar al pecho
Y ser latidos de nubes sobre otras regiones

Después de los ojos alegres
Vienen los ojos tristes
Después de las alas cercanas
Vienen las alas olientes a distancias
Vienen y se llevan la memoria
La memoria que quiere alejarse del cuerpo
Los números de las meses
Que no tienen corazón para subir un poco
Los números de los años
Que no tienen color por el llanto que los borra
Los nombres de las flores
Que se quedan atrás de su perfume
Que recuerdan tus manos y las buscan
Entre cielo y tierra

[MY LIPS TRY TO LEAVE MY MOUTH]

My lips try to leave my mouth
To run elsewhere
Boasting of infinity
My heartbeat intends to leave my chest
And be the heartbeat of clouds above other parts

After the cheerful eyes
Come sad eyes
After the nearby wings
Come wings that can be smelled from a distances
They come and take the memory away
The memory that wants to leave the body
The numbers of months
That don't have the heart to rise a little
The numbers of years
That have no colour because of the weeping that erases them
The names of flowers
That linger behind their scent
That remember your hands and go in search of them
Between heaven and earth

[ÉRAMOS LOS ELEGIDOS DEL SOL]

Éramos los elegidos del sol
Y no nos dimos cuenta
Fuimos los elegidos de lo más alta estrella
Y no supimos responder a su regalo
Angustia de impotencia
El agua nos amaba
La tierra nos amaba
Las selvas eran nuestras
El éxtasis era nuestro espacio propio
Tu mirada era el universo frente a frente
Tu belleza era el sonido del amanecer
La primavera amada por los árboles
Ahora somos una tristeza contagiosa
Una muerte antes de tiempo
El alma que no sabe en qué sitio se encuentra
El invierno en los huesos sin un relámpago
Y todo esto porque tú no supiste lo que es la eternidad
Ni comprendiste el alma de mi alma en su barco de tinieblas
En su trono de águila herida de infinito

[WE WERE THE CHOSEN OF THE SUN]

We were the chosen of the sun
And we did not realise
We were chosen by the highest star
And we did not know how to respond to its gift
Distress at our impotence
The water loved us
The earth loved us
The forests were ours
Ecstasy was our very own space
Your gaze was face to face with the universe
Your beauty was the sound of dawn
The springtime loved by trees
Now we are a contagious sadness
A death before its time
The soul that knows not where it is
Winter in the bones with no lightning bolt
And all this because you did not know what eternity is
Nor did you understand the soul of my soul in its ship of darkness
On its throne of an eagle wounded by infinity

[ABRAMOS NUESTRO PECHO]

Abramos nuestro pecho
Para que el cielo se reconozca
Ayudemos a la tierra a sostenerse
A ser grandeza en su manto de recuerdos
Y no simple navío en marcha
Que ella sea el pensamiento que la eleva
Que sea el sentirse a sí misma
El sufrimiento que arraiga hasta debajo de las tumbas

Brotan los ríos para hallarse solos
Nacen los árboles y las casas de los hombres
Se forman razas buscando une flor maravillosa
El mar se mueve para que no lo olviden
Todo anhela una dulce comprensión admirativa
Dónde está el hombre y el fundamento oscuro
En dónde está la desventura la voluntad y el ansia
Y él aparece en su razón de ser
Qué buscas hombre de mirada variable
Algo que se ha perdido entre los siglos
Algo que era nuestro y demasiado grande
Tan esencia de todo que no supimos ver
Y se nos fue en tinieblas vida abajo

[LET US OPEN OUR BOSOM]

Let us open our bosom
So that the heavens might repent
Let us help the earth to keep going
To achieve greatness in its cloak of memories
And not just a moving ship
May it be the thought that raises it
May it be the sense of its own self
The suffering that takes root beneath graves

Rivers gush forth only to find themselves alone
Trees and the houses of men are born
Strains are developed in the search for a wonderful flower
The sea moves so as not to be forgotten
Everything longs for sweet admiring understanding
Where is man and his dark foundations
Where is misfortune free will and desire
And he appears in his raison d'être
Oh man with the fickle gaze what do you seek
Something that has been lost amongst the ages
Something that was ours and too great
So much the essence of everything that we could not see it
And it left us in darkness life laid low

SEA COMO SEA

Siempre serán les flores en su risa
Como anuncio de amor y mariposa a nado
Como irradiación de recuerdos
La luna destrozada que se aleja
Los sitios de silencio convertidos en obra
Esperanza instantánea
En las miradas con sus cerros
Y sus animales pastando
¿De dónde viene tanta semilla tanto instinto
Tanto deseo de abrazo y de prodigio?

Los pájaros sueñan por nosotros
La flor ansiada duerme en los sótanos del mar
Sólo tenemos esta cascada que apaga a los fantasmas
Estas piedras escondiéndose bajo el ala
Entre los girasoles que se insultan como colegiales
Sólo tenemos el corazón de paso a paso
Los sonidos para causar el aire que se creía libre
Las estatuas para los relámpagos

Cuando viene la tarde amasando sus panes
El imán de las rosas atrae los navíos
El río inunda a las ovejas atraviesa los ojos
Y se quiebra al fondo de la soledad
Cuando viene el silencio hipnotizando selvas
Las rocas se lanzan de cabeza al fondo de las aguas
Lo que hace llorar a las novias más lejanas
El viento peina a los rebaños
Arroje su capa y huye para siempre
Les perfumes de las flores mueren y sus colores nacen
Lo que hace ladrar a los perros al pie de la colina

BE THAT AS IT MAY

There will always be flowers in her laughter
Like a declaration of love and floating butterflies
Like exposure of memories
The shattered moon that moves away
Places of silence turned into works of art
Immediate hope
In those views with their hills
And their animals grazing
Where do so many seeds come from so much instinct
So much desire for embraces and wonder?

Birds dream for us
The long-awaited flower sleeps in the sea's vaults
All we have is this waterfall extinguishing phantoms
These stones hiding under a wing
Amongst sunflowers that call one another names like schoolboys
We only have courage one step at a time
Sounds to stir the air that was thought to be free
Statues for lightning bolts

When evening comes kneading its bread
The rose magnet attracts ships
The river overruns the sheep passes through their eyes
And breaks up in the depths of loneliness
When silence arrives hypnotising forests
Rocks are thrown head first into the water's depths
Which causes the most distant brides to weep
The wind combs the flocks
Throws off its cape and flees forever
The scent from the flowers dies away and their colours appear
Which makes dogs bark at the bottom of the hill

Y nada más
Una avenida de parientes de cadenas
De ahorcados de luces fugitivas
De barcos en peligro entre dos astros

And nothing more
An avenue of relatives in chains
Of men hanged from fugitive lights
Of vessels in danger between two stars

[EL AÑO SURCABA LOS AIRES]

El año surcaba los aires en sus meses
Como el himno devorando las olas extasiadas
Flor traslúcida en sus barcos de vida o muerte
Nada vas a decirnos que no sepamos como tú
Las líneas de las manos son inútiles
Y asimismo las líneas de batalla
Digamos a los ojos que tanto han devorado
Que aun hay algo nuevo o que podría serlo

[THE YEAR PLOUGHED THE AIR]

The year ploughed the air throughout its months
Like a hymn devouring ecstatic waves
Translucent flower on its vessels of life or death
You cannot tell us anything we don't know as well as you
The lines on one's hands are useless
And lines of battle equally so
Let us tell the eyes that have devoured so much
That there is still something new or that there might be

[LEJANÍA DE MURMULLOS]

Lejanía de murmullos
De viejos ríos amados
Que quieren cambiar de cauce
Cielo de ansias y de astros
Y de estrellas maniatadas

[REMOTE MURMURS]

Remote murmurs
Of beloved old rivers
That want to change course
Sky of longings and heavenly bodies
And handcuffed stars

CAMBIO AL HORIZONTE

Un hombre de amanecer y laurel acogido
Con grandes distancias en la vez
Y sueños migratorios en cada parte de su carne
Un hombre del despertar en cuyo pecho
Murieron los sutiles sonidos del antaño cerrado
Y se rehace el mundo en escalas sin lágrimas
Y se alumbra en sus manos a medida que va naciendo
Un hombre de estrellas libertadas
Va cantando como un navío
Los pájaros cruzan el cielo desde hace tantos siglos
Y el mundo suena bajo las olas hermanas

Un hombre de ayer viene hacia hoy
Trae la oscuridad a cuestas como una melodía
Y busca el cetro del resplandor en la punta de sus ojos
Con su ansiosa mirada que humedece el espacio
De este planeta triste y sin excusa
Un hombre de ayer trae una substancia de miedos
De seculares odios brotando por sus cabellos
De recuerdos enanos rodando por sus miradas
Un hombre de ayer viene hacia hoy
Y es preciso enseñarle los caminos nacientes
Como una canción que se agranda
Y se llena de cosas imprevistas
Hombre de amanecer que se mira las manos
Y encuentra las raíces de futuros paisajes

Enseña tus mármoles contra la tempestad
Construye tus grandes torres contra la bruma silenciosa
Danos tus luces furibundos
Y golpea la larva de los astros venideros
Con la voz de la vida que te enciende les alas
Un hombre de amanecer y de lámpara abrupta

CHANGE OF HORIZON

A man of dawn and laurels welcomed
With great distances at the same time
And migratory dreams in every part of his flesh
A man alert in whose breast
The subtle sounds of past ages died away
And the world is rebuilt in stages without any tears
And lights up in his hands while there emerges
A man with liberated stars
Who goes singing like a ship
Birds have been crossing the sky for so many centuries
And the world echoes beneath the brotherly waves

A man from yesterday approaches today
Brings darkness on his back like a melody
And seeks the radiant sceptre at the tip of his eyes
With their anxious gaze dampening the space
Of this sad and unapologetic planet
A man from yesterday brings a wealth of fears
Of secular hatreds springing from his hair
Of dwarf memories rolling along before their eyes
A man from yesterday approaches today
And needs to be taught the emerging pathways
Like a song that gets longer
And is filled with unexpected things
Man of dawn who looks at his hands
And finds the roots of future landscapes

Train your marble against the storm
Build your great towers against the silent mist
Give us your furious lights
And strike the larvae of approaching stars
With the voice of life that lights up your wings
A man of dawn and sudden torches

Sobre su caballo henchido de relinchos
Como una paloma apasionada
Va alumbrando la vida de pensamientos atados a su entusiasmo

Y va subiendo subiendo del día hacia la noche
Y se queda un instante parado en su nombre
Cuando las campanas alimentan el aire de la noche
El hombre de ayer se va sintiendo un poco muerto
Y un poco corazón sin objeto
No sabe cual es la hora ni que tiempo se adorna en su sitio preciso
Contempla el año triste que va pasando bajo el cielo
Los árboles hacen un ruido de hombres dolorosos
Tiembla en su alma de torbellinos lentos y recorre la noche
Como un suspiro llevado de mano
Es preciso enseñarle nuestro mundo
La canción que se agranda y se llena de horizontes
Es preciso que aprenda a abrir caminos
Que ascienda como esas plantas que perecen tener alas
Que sepa que se trata de atraer las lejanías
Y que deben tenerlas en sus adentros
Que nos reímos de la noche que se estrella en los torres
Cuando los árboles se cansan de querer escalar el cielo
Es preciso que aprenda la amistad de la luz
Y el buen sentido de las manos unidas como flores poderosas

(De lo contrario deberemos cortarle la cabeza debajo de la barba todos
    sus hilos en relación con las estrellas)

On his horse that burst into snorts
Like a passionate dove
He is lighting up the life of thoughts tethered to his zeal

And he keeps going up and up from day into night
And stands still for a moment on his behalf
When the bells feed the night-time air
The man from yesterday leaves feeling a little dead
And a little like an aimless heart
He knows not what time it is nor what time is glorified where he stands
He beholds the sad year passing beneath the sky
Trees make sounds like men in distress
He trembles in his soul of slow whirlwinds and tours the night
Like a hand-held sigh
He needs to be taught about our world
About the song that gets longer and is filled with horizons
He needs to learn to open up pathways
May he rise like those worn-out plants that seem to have wings
May he know that it is all about luring distances
And that they have to keep them in their hearts
That we mock the night that crashes into the towers
When the trees tire of wanting to climb up to the sky
One needs to learn the friendship of light
And the good sense of hands joined like powerful flowers

(Otherwise we will have to cut off his head below the beard all of its
    strands connected to the stars)

DE CUANDO EN CUANDO

Viene en suspirada tarde
Con un número de latidos para mirar su lago
Oye caer su peso vida abajo
Encuentra estrellas en cualquier tumba
En cualquier llave olvidada por la selva

Viene con ojos de repertorio
En olas escogidas por su finura
Se detiene en su nombre
Se mira las manos más allá del planeta
En la noche de la distancia
Solloza de puro mar
Habla haciendo praderas
En su dulce planeta arrojado a los perros

Viene callada en cementerio de ebriedades
Y sabe que está lloviendo sobre su nombre
Como el crecer de un cielo impenetrable
Viene recoge sus miradas
Y se va contra el viento del medio

FROM TIME TO TIME

He arrives late with a sigh
And for several heartbeats he observes the lake
Hears his load falling down through life
Finds stars in any grave whatever
In whatever key forgotten by the forest

He arrives with repertory eyes
On waves selected for their fineness
He pauses at his name
Observes his hands on the other side of the planet
During the night of distance
Sobs over fresh seas
Speaks of making pastures
On his sweet planet tossed to the dogs

Silence arrives inebriated in the graveyard
And knows it is raining on his name
As if an impenetrable sky is growing
He takes back his eyes
And sets off from the centre into the wind

BELLAS PROMESAS

Palabra que desata su palomo
El llanto huele sus playas y las noches movedizas
Encuentra allí un recuerdo como el espejo de las islas
Unos pies olvidados por el viento derecho
Yo he de seguir por las miradas del ciego
Mar adentro grito afuera
Tomando la forma del furor
Y la gracia de los espectros en su tiempo

Un castillo en el aire ronca toda la noche
Tú sientes las hojas de los muertos
Y lo que eres en los sueñes cuando la edad se abre
Cuando la sombra apaga la sed de los caballos
Los árboles marcan el paso
La visita del peligro inunda los sentidos
Y el bosque aguarda respirando apenas

Has olvidado el corazón en sus vientos de estrella
Sus noches voladoras entre pájaros desbordados
La espuma de la sangre en su silencio de oro
La luna que predica en el desierto

Un castillo en el aire escupo sobre los hombres
La eternidad se abre en el pavor de su presencia
Este es el eco sin orillas
Los espacios cruzados por los siglos
El insomnio de los ríos ilustres
Los muebles que crujen al viajar en sueños
El ruido de la calle que se peina en el espejo

Castillos en el aire y en el tiempo devorando luces
Manos ansiosas y escalas fugitivas
Los pechos rompen en arroyos

FINE PROMISES

Word that untethers its dove
The tears smell of their beaches and of restless nights
Find a souvenir there like a mirror from the islands
Some feet forgotten by the derecho windstorm
I have to follow the blind man's gaze
Offshore I let out a scream
Taking the shape of rage
And the grace of wraiths in their time

A castle in the air snores all night long
You feel the leaves of the dead
And whatever you are in dreams when the era is revealed
When the shadow quenches the horses' thirst
The trees keep in step
The arrival of danger floods the senses
And the forest waits scarcely breathing

You have forgotten the heart in its starry winds
Its flying nights amongst overwhelming birds
The foam of blood in its golden silence
The moon preaching in the desert

A castle in the air spits on men
Eternity opens up dreading its presence
This is the echo with no shores
Space crossed by centuries
The insomnia of illustrious rivers
Furniture creaking when travelling in dreams
The noise from the street combing its hair in the mirror

Castles in the air and in time devouring lights
Anxious hands and unstable ladders
Breasts burst into streams

Para que crezcan los rebaños en su lamento
Este tiene una atmósfera de piedra
Aquel un horizonte propio con ruedas suaves para la noche

Voz de olvido y silencio dejado de la mano
Para las lágrimas detenidas
Para las llaves del abismo a nuestra espalda
Los años pasan como selvas
Las mariposas vuelan de los ojos del muerto

So that the lamentations of the flocks might increase
This one has a stony atmosphere
That one its own horizon with smooth wheels for night-time

Voice of oblivion and forsaken silence
For the blocked tears
For the keys to the abyss at our backs
The years go by like forests
Butterflies fly from the dead man's eyes

LA MANO DEL INSTANTE

Igual destello de hierbas provisorias
De árboles escritos a diez ojos a la redonda
Igual ahora de viento y crujido de párpados
Igual entonces de lluvias preferidas a los ríos
A causa del sentimiento que cae
A diez ojos a la redonda

En esta hora se queman las esperas
Se cortan los pedazos de miradas
Vienen las orillas a hablarnos en secreto
Y se cierran las olas con gran ruido
Todo está preparado de largo tiempo
El alma desciende a sus venenos
Los paseantes buscan su golondrina hipnotizada
Descargan sus países
Y se alejan por el ruido de sus pasos
En esta hora de destellos iguales
A diez ejes a la redonda
Se muere el cielo de su leche ordeñada
El mar no quiere decir ni una palabra más
Yo quiero decir montaña y digo árbol

Igual destello de ojos en lontananza
Igual ternura de caballos en el aire
Igual entonces de rosas meritorias
Igual por qué de palomas en su violín
Igual eternidad de escalas en sueños ascendentes

THE HAND AT THAT MOMENT

The same glimmer of temporary herbs
From trees written in a ten-eye radius
The same now for wind and creaking eyelids
The same then for rains preferred to rivers
Because of the feeling that falls
In a ten-eye radius

At this time hopes burn up
Stares are cut into pieces
The shores come to speak with us in secret
And the waves close up with a great crash
Everything has been ready so long
The soul descends with its venom
Passers-by seek its hypnotized swallow
Offload their countries
And are driven away by the sound of their footsteps
At this time of equal flickers
In a ten-axle radius
The sky dies from fresh milk
The sea will not say one word more
I mean mountain but I say tree

The same glimmering eyes in the background
The same tender horses in the air
The same then for deserving roses
The same is true of doves in his violin
The same never-ending ladders in ascending dreams

ESTRELLA HIJA DE ESTRELLA

Había signos en el aire
Había presagios en el cielo
Tenía que brotar la gracia de repente
Con sus pasos de gloria
Con todos sus gérmenes sagrados
Con su aliento de vida o muerte

Venía la belleza de quien sabe dónde
Venía hacía mis ojos
Con su andar de planeta seguro de su tiempo
Es la ley misteriosa que de pronto se encarna
Y se hace realidad en un instante

El azar se presenta
Con todas sus fuerzas invencibles
El azar con sus constelaciones desatadas
Que súbito se anudan
Para cumplir con un destino entre las piedras lentas
El aire vibra de los sonidos de la vieja flauta
Una dulce amistad ha nacido en el mundo
Acaso un gran peligro se yergue de su noche

La voz de un hombre dice Estrella
Y tiembla como una estrella
El viento pasa y el azul amado
Deja caer su aroma
Para ungir las cabezas señaladas

Ahí viene sobre dos pies alados
Envuelta de música de nardos y de bosques
La gracia y la belleza
Entre los ruidos de las calles
Sobre sus pies alados

STAR CHILD OF STAR

There were signs in the air
There were omens in the sky
Mercy had to spring forth all at once
With its footsteps in glory
With all its sacred seeds
With its breath of life or death

There came the beauty from who knows where
She approached my eyes
Secure in her rhythm with a planetary trajectory
She is the mysterious law that suddenly takes shape
And becomes reality in an instant

Chance turns up
With all its invincible forces
Chance with its constellations unleashed
How suddenly they are knotted together
To fulfil a destiny amongst slow stones
The air vibrates with the sound of the old flute
A sweet friendship has been conceived in the world
Perhaps a great danger arises from its night

A man's voice says Star
And trembles like a star
The wind passes and the beloved sky
Lets its scent fall
To anoint distinguished heads

There she comes on two winged feet
Wrapped in the music of tuberoses and woodlands
Grace and beauty
Amongst the sounds of the streets
On her winged feet

Aparece de pronto entre los hombres y las casas
Y todo cae en el vacío
Los ruidos las casas y las calles
Como las ropas de una mujer que se desnuda
Sólo tú quedas en el mundo
Sólo tu cuerpo como una flor inmensa
Que llena el universo

¡Oh tierra cómo te has hecho bella en un instante!

Dos miradas se cruzan
Y canta un árbol nuevo
Dos manos se entrelazan
Dos anhelos se encuentran
Dos angustias se hablan en secreto
¿Por qué razón?
Sólo los signos y el azar lo saben
Dos corazones reconocen un impulso ciego
Y el camino que abre al infinito

Un hombre dice Estrella
Y hay un temblor en los espacios
Un hombre dice Mar
Y las olas se agrandan satisfechas
Un hombre dice Selva
Y los árboles comprenden su deber milenario
Un hombre dice Viento
Y todo se agita hasta la muerte

Estrella yo no te pido tu destino
Ni exijo más aroma a la flor de la tarde
Yo quiero sólo una amistad de anchas orillas
Un gran río profundo
Que embruje mis paisajes
Y haga cantar las aguas adormiladas
Que siempre creen olvidar su vida

She appears suddenly amongst the people and houses
And everything falls into the void
The noise the houses and the streets
Like the clothes of a woman getting undressed
Only you are left in the world
Only your body like an enormous flower
Filling the universe

O earth how beautiful you have become in no time at all!

Two gazes intersect
And a new tree sings
Two hands intertwine
Two desires meet
Two anxieties are spoken of in secret
Why is that?
Only the stars and destiny know why
Two hearts recognize a blind urge
And the path that opens to infinity

A man says Star
And there is a quake in space
A man says Sea
And the waves swell up in satisfaction
A man says Forest
And the trees understand their age-old duty
A man says Wind
And everything is shaken to death

Star I do not ask for your fate
Nor do I demand more scent from the evening flower
I want only a friendship with wide shores
A great deep river
May it bewitch my countryside
And make the drowsy waters sing
Which always think they have forgotten their lives

La calle del azar el punto mismo
Donde se encuentran los designios

Los ojos se adivinan
Se entornan suaves en un sueño
Saben que juntos van a mirar las cosas
Los labios se presienten
Palpitan como flores que empiezan la jornada
¿Son besos? ¿Son palabras?
¿Es un cambio de ideas a través de los años?

Por qué llegas tan tarde a mi jardín
Por qué no apresuraste la marcha en las tinieblas
Con qué derecho el tiempo
Separa la flor del árbol que era suyo
Por qué pone distancias en los años
No sabes que este trozo de tierra te aguardaba
Cansado de cantar y de llamarte

Yo te había elegido
Como la tierra al árbol de su gracia
Como el naufragio el barco más amado
Esto es grande y es triste
Porque no hay modo de cambiar los signos
Mi exaltación acaso te asustaba
Ella era real como las tempestades
Perdónalo que venga y es que ya ha nacido
No es culpe mía si el destino habla

Entre el cielo y la tierra
Hay algo grande que comienza
Tierra y cielo sienten temblar las rocas y las nubes
Cielo y tierra son cómplices del sueño
Y sus pájaros nacientes sin permiso
¿Serás mi estrella
Entre la vida y la muerte sorprendida?

The street of chance the same point
At which designs may be found

The eyes can be made out
They are curled up peacefully in a dream
They know that together they will be observing things
The lips have a premonition
They pulsate like flowers at the beginning of the day
Are those kisses? Are those words?
Is this an exchange of ideas over the years?

Why do you arrive so late in my garden
Why did you not hasten your progress in the darkness
By what right does time
Separate the flower from the tree that was its own
Why does it put distance into the years
Do you not know that this piece of land awaited you
Weary of singing and calling for you

I had chosen you
As did the earth its favoured tree
As did the shipwreck the most beloved vessel
This one is large and it is sad
Because there is no way to change the signs
Perhaps my elation frightened you
It was as real as the storms
Forgive it for coming and for having already emerged
It is not my fault if destiny speaks

Between heaven and earth
There something great has been set in motion
Earth and sky feel the rocks and the clouds shudder
Heaven and earth are dream's accomplices
And their birds born without permission
Will you be my star
Caught unawares between life and death?

Ven hacia mí más mía que mis huesos
Ven entre mirtos y mármoles profundos
Oh cuerpo del ritmo eterno
Oh la amistad de músicas y cielos infinitos
Oh belleza del mundo
Permíteme acordarme de mí mismo

Come to me you who are more mine than my own bones
Come amongst myrtles and deep marble
O body of eternal rhythm
O the friendship of music and infinite skies
O beauty of the world
Allow me to remember my own self

PALABRAS DE LA DANZA

Tierra de ritmo aéreo
Sangre raza escalonada hacia arriba
Profundidad geológica saliendo a luz en armonía
Células de antigua carne en nueva etapa
Tierra tierra para su cielo y traspasar su cielo
Hasta la negra nada giratoria y la locura del universo

Este gran torbellino de fuego originario y fuentes vivas
Este cuerpo de viento en su horizonte puro
No cae de su cumbre al drama sin razón precisa
Significa la luz herida gravemente

La paloma sonámbula
El árbol que sueña que se está ahogando
La piedra que rueda y cambia de planeta
Significa el despertar de las edades
El camino hacia adentro con sus ejércitos de hormigas
Que empiezan a cantar para subir de rango
Con su sangre que se pierde de vista
Antes de caer la noche
Con sus entrañas en lo más profundo
En lo anterior a todo pensamiento y la blancura misma
Significa hipnotizar los siglos y las montañas y los mares
Llegar en un delirio de veranos entre polo y polo
Con los ojos pletóricos
Levantar sus abismos en los brazos
Y morirse de sol sobre la hierba

Dice el torrente en vértigo de nubes y regiones
Aquí estoy para el triunfo de las viejas soledades
De las tumbas remotas que aprenden a volar

WORDS FROM THE DANCE

Land of airy rhythm
Blood lineage stepped upwards
Geological depth coming to light in harmony
Cells from old flesh at a new stage
Earth earth for its sky and piercing its sky
Until the black spinning void and the madness of the universe

This great whirlwind of original fire and living fountains
This body of wind on its pure horizon
Does not fall from its summit into drama for no exact reason
This means the light is seriously injured

The sleepwalking dove
The tree that dreams it is drowning
The stone rolling by and changing planets
Means that the ages are being awoken
The way into the interior with its armies of ants
That begin singing so as to rise in rank
With their blood lost from sight
Before nightfall
With their essence in the furthest depths
Preceding all thought and the very whiteness
This means hypnotizing the centuries and the mountains and the seas
To arrive in delirious summers between pole and pole
With elated eyes
To raise the chasms in their arms
And die on the grass in the sun

The stream says in dizzying clouds and regions
Here I am for the triumph of old solitudes
Of remote tombs that are learning to fly

Aquí estoy entre los pueblos respirando
Sobre arenas calientes que se mueven
Aquí estoy con la fascinación de las esferas
En substancia de anhelos perdidos en la noche
Aquí estoy para atar el día a mis caderas
Y que la edad de piedra sea la edad de oro
Espantando las lágrimas que pudieran quemarse
Arrojando el dolor a sus eclipses solidarios

Aquí estoy como una perla errante en los espacios
Para tus vendavales infinitos
Y tu cráter abierto a su primer suspiro

Here I am breathing amongst the people
On hot shifting sands
Here I am with a fascination for the spheres
With a wealth of desire lost in the night
Here I am to tie the day to my hips
And may the stone age be the golden age
Scaring away tears that might dry up
Throwing sorrow at their shared eclipses

Here I am like a pearl wandering in space
For your infinite rainy seasons
And your crater open for its first breath

TIEMPO-ESPACIO

Yo estaba sobre el tiempo
Sentado sobre el tiempo
Como un astro de flores y volcanes
Acaso como un dios o más bien un poeta
Veía pasar siluetas de dominios cometas y torrentes
Allá arriba entre silencias devorantes
Veía rostros estropeados en mi vida
Al fondo de un estanque que abre y cierra los ojos
Oía el correr del cielo entre sus dos orillas
Las estrelles que se fueron para no volver
Abajo hay cierta pretensión de vida
Fantasma de deseo de angustias y problemas en llamas
Espejos fascinantes como un bosque que se hunde en la arena
Hay barcos crecedores en los atardeceres
Igual que los muertos que se llevan
Hay suspiros como quien se ahoga en su música interna
Hay la vida que quiere ser vida
El día que se envenena con su luz excesiva
La noche como uno que llora
El cielo como uno que canta
La tierra como uno que anda
El mar como el que se esconde debajo de la mesa
Y luego por sobre todo y bajo todo
El espacio que quiere avenirse con el tiempo
El tiempo que no acepta insinuaciones

TIME-SPACE

I was above time
Seated above time
Like a star of flowers and volcanoes
Perhaps like a god or better still a poet
I watched silhouettes of domains comets and floods passing by
Up there amongst devouring silences
During my life I saw ruined faces
At the bottom of a pond that opens and closes its eyes
I heard the sky running between its two shores
The stars that left never to return
Down here there is a certain pretence at life
Phantom of desire of anguish and problems ablaze
Fascinating mirrors like a forest sinking into the sand
There are ships able to grow in the sunset
Just like the dead they take with them
There are sighs like those from one drowning in his inner music
There is life that wants to be life
The day it is poisoned by its excessive light
The night like one who weeps
The sky like one who sings
The earth like one who walks
The sea like the man hiding under the table
And then above all and under all
Space that wants to come to terms with time
Time that accepts no insinuations

[VEO EL UNIVERSO REDUCIDO]

Veo el universo reducido
A una caja entre cirios y flores que se despiden
Me veo y veo a tantos otros
Ovejas de amargura
Sobre el abrevadero de tu ataúd
Bebiendo la eternidad y su belleza

Pobrecitas palomas malheridas
Lavando en la muerte
Su sangre y su dolor de muerte

Así estuvimos así estaremos
Grabados para siempre
En el recuerdo y su gran llaga
Y hemos de vernos siempre corderos desolados
Bebiendo tu dulzura y contando los minutos del [silencio]*
En qué mares se mece este ataúd
Con su velamen pronto
Zarpamos todos   Por qué tú sola
Yo mecía tu cuna de la muerte
Como un día meciste la cuna de mi vida
Mecía tu ataúd hecho un jardín
Lleno de rosas vestidas de viaje
Sobre las olas de la angustia
Oía cantar las aguas niñas hacia el sol
Y detrás de los rosales
Veía tu rostro y tu sonrisa
Como si te pasearas muy alegre
Tu sola satisfecha
En un planeta de llantos

---

* *Después de las palabras* "minutos del" *sigue una palabra ilegible en el manuscrito. El editor de la* Obra poética *propone la lectura* "silencio".

[I SEE THE UNIVERSE REDUCED]

I see the universe reduced
To a box amongst candles and flowers bidding farewell
I see myself and so many others
Bitter sheep
At your coffin's watering hole
Drinking of eternity and its beauty

Poor little doves badly wounded
Washing away in death
Their blood and their death-pains

Thus we were thus we will be
Engraved forever
In memory and its great wound
And we must always see one another as forlorn lambs
Drinking your sweetness and counting the minutes of [silence]*
On what seas does this coffin rock
With its sails at the ready
Shall we all set sail   Why you alone
I rocked your cradle of death
As one day you rocked the cradle of my life
I rocked your coffin made a garden
Full of roses dressed for travel
On waves of anxiety
I heard the child-like waters singing to the sun
And behind the rose bushes
I saw your face and your smile
As if you were strolling cheerfully
You alone satisfied
On a planet of tears

---

* After "minutes of the" there follows an illegible word in the manuscript. The editor of the Poetic Works suggests it should read "silence".

Por qué embarcaste sola en ese barco
Y te sonríes?
Crujen las jarcias de tu velero
Conoces al piloto que arrojó el corazón a los tiburones
Y mira el hoyo en el pecho vacío
Como los ojos de los ciegos
Qué barco es éste que tiene tanta prisa
Que desgarra les andas de nuestro corazón
Y corta todas las amarras
Qué fantasma nocturno irguió las velas
De dónde viene ese viento
Que te lleva como si fueras suya
Pero no sabe que eres mía?
Que me estés escrita en las entrañas
Que estás hirviendo en mi garganta
Que barco es éste que no teme tantas lágrimas
Que no se asusta de los sollozos
Ni de los huracanes de nuestro pecho
Qué barco es éste que viene a desafiarme
Oh marinero negro
No conoces mi fuerza de rebelde
Ignores mi soberbia de monstruo arcaico

Why did you board that ship alone
And then smile?
Your vessel's rigging creaks
You know the pilot who threw his heart to the sharks
And look at the hole there in his empty chest
Like blind men's eyes
What boat is this that is in such a hurry
That rips the coffin-stands from our heart
And cuts all moorings
What nocturnal phantom raised the sails
Where does that wind come from
Which carries you off as if you belonged to it
But does not know that you are mine?
That you are inscribed on my soul
That you are boiling in my throat
What boat is this that is not afraid of so many tears
That does not fear the sobbing
Nor the hurricanes in our bosom
What boat is this that comes to challenge me
Oh dark sailor
You do not recognise my stubborn strength
You are not aware of my monstrous archaic pride

EL PASAJERO DE SU DESTINO

1

Es así como somos
Y como nos paseamos hoy sobre la tierra
Precedidos por los ruidos de nuestros antepasados y seguidos por el
        dolor de nuestros hijos
Aferrados a nuestra edad y cantando cuando las rocas lloran la muerte
        de un velero que han preferido sin razón alguna
O tal vez porque lo vieron jugar en su infancia
O porque era hermoso todo lleno de viento viniendo del país del viento

No tenemos miedo cuando el viento arranca las palabras de nuestra garganta
No tenemos miedo de las ballenas ni de todos esos monstruos que
        tienen más envergadura que una campanada
No tenemos miedo de inclinarnos sobre vuestras canciones de las cuales
        pueden saltar un geyser amenazador y el vértigo infinito de las brumas
No tenemos miedo del más allá que va a saltar sobre nuestra razón

Y de ese frío lúcido que vela sobre la constelación de nuestras inquietudes
Más absurdo que el muerto que han encerrado con la mitad de una carta
        en el cerebro
Con una palabra fabulosa en medio de la lengua
Con un gran rostro entre dos hilos de lágrimas al fondo de sus ojos
Esos ojos que se convertirán en tiernos guijarros sobre los caminos del
        más allá
Todo esto es útil para la formación de la superficie
Para el interés del fuego impaciente en el fondo de su antro
Y debernos señalar su trabajo y elogiar su ley

Es tarde en todos los rincones del mundo
Es tarde y el tarde va a hundirse en el mar
Sin soltar el timón del horizonte
Porque él es el jefe único él guarda el secreto
El puede levantar el brazo y desatar de la muerte el cadáver reciente

PASSENGER OF HIS DESTINY

1

That is how we are now
And how we walk the earth today
Preceded by the sounds of our ancestors and followed by the sorrow of
    our children
Clinging to our age and singing when rocks mourn the death of a
    sailing boat that they favoured for no reason whatsoever
Or perhaps it was because they saw it playing as a child
Or because it was beautiful all full of wind coming from the land of winds

We have no fear when the wind blows the words from our throats
We have no fear of whales nor of all those monsters with wingspans
    greater than a peal of bells
We have no fear of concentrating on your songs from which a menacing
    geyser and the infinite vertigo of mists might gush forth
We have no fear of the hereafter that will leap over our reason

And that lucid cold that watches over the constellation of our worries
More absurd than the dead man they have locked up with half a letter in
    his brain
With one fabulous word at the centre of his tongue
With a great face between two threads of tears deep in his eyes
Those eyes that will turn into tender pebbles on the paths of the hereafter
All this is useful for shaping the surface
For interesting the impatient fire deep in its den
And we should mention its work and praise its law

It is late in every corner of the world
It is late and the late afternoon is about to sink into the sea
Without releasing the horizon's rudder
Because it is the sole master it keeps the secret
It can raise an arm and untether fresh corpses from death

Ahora que tú tiemblas como el mar
El horizonte va a hundirse para siempre
Ahora que la selva se pasa al enemigo
Lánzate sobre el mar
Separando las olas como el cadáver separa la eternidad

Hombre tú ves que el mar se amalgama y tienes miedo
Tú bien podrías saltar por encima de la conflagración de mentiras unánimes
Invade el terreno sideral sin vacilar
Invade los países del loco que te desprecia y te mira con la parte inferior
        de su alma
Proclama tu importancia a la tribu sometida que empieza a aparecer en
        el fondo del cielo

II

La tierra está en fiebre a causa de los cantos seculares de los pájaros
Es el despertar inútil de la tribu iluminándose a cada paso
El mar lava sus olas sus olas que deben suavizar el mundo
Y esparcir sus caricias hasta la extinción de la comarca
Es probable que vayan a pulir el cielo como la proa de un gran navío
Tal vez envejezcan antes que les árboles obsesionados por fantasmas
        después da medianoche
Los árboles sin suerte los árboles perdidos como el abuelo que trata de
        salir de nuestra profundidad
Y hacer gestos de ausencia en el vacío
He aquí el acontecimiento abrupto después de la perdición
He ahí la habitual desdicha del que no puede detener los ríos

Y debe llorar sus muertes como las montañas
En vano él quisiera cerrar el mar
Mañana les espumas emitirán un pensamiento nuevo
Harán coronas brillantes para mi corazón capaz de rodar como vuestros
        mejores veleros
La catástrofe memorable huye sin esperar el resultado
Se hunde a velas desplegadas en las aguas antiguas

Now that you tremble like the sea
The horizon is going to sink once and for all
Now that the forest is going over to the enemy
Throw yourself into the sea
Dividing the waves the way a corpse divides eternity

Man you see that the seas merge and you are afraid
You may as well jump over the conflagration of unanimous lies
Invade the celestial sphere with no hesitation
Invade the lands of the madman who despises you and watches you with
    the lesser part of his soul
Proclaim your importance to the subdued tribe that starts to appear in
    the furthest reaches of the sky

II

The earth is in a fever because of the secular songs of birds
It is the useless awakening of the tribe lighting up with every step
The sea washes its waves its waves that should soften the world
And scatters endearments until the region's demise
It is likely they will polish the sky like the prow of a great ship
Perhaps they will grow old before the ghost-obsessed trees after midnight
The unfortunate trees the trees lost like an ancestor trying to emerge
    from our depths
Making gestures of absence in the void
Here we have the sudden event following the downfall
There we have the usual misfortune of one unable to hold rivers back

And it must mourn their death like the mountains
In vain would it like to seal off the sea
Tomorrow the surf will express a new thought
Will make bright crowns for my heart capable of steering like your finest
    sailing boats
The memorable catastrophe flees without waiting for the result
It sinks under full sail in the ancient waters

Sin siquiera mirar al rey a la deriva que ha olvidado las maniobras de
  excepción
He visto como nadie surgir bajo mis pies la abierta soledad
Y he sentido en mis ojos el sobresalto estelar
El tal vez idéntico a los parajes desconocidos
La lejanía sin solución
El sitio de la altura en dónde alguien ha dejado la huella de sus pies
La punta extrema del árbol en donde empieza el infinito
Y el mar a lo lejos como el terror de la noche
Silencio os suplico silencio
Hay un sueño que pasa entre los hombres
Hay un sueño en marcha entre les hombres y los presagios
Tenemos sed de un sitio sin inquietud y sin cálculo
En donde el demonio de la tempestad tendrá los ojos marchitos y los
  cabellos cortados
Silencio te suplico
Mira pasar la nave hipnotizada de mi alma
Arrastrando una larga barba de agua
Mira esa estrella en el fondo del cielo
Esa estrella que se aleja con todos sus marineros

III

Es preciso arrojar los números y seguirlos con nuestros ojos
Verlos tomar su puesto buscar la elevación injusta del humo
O bien caer al fondo de la memoria
Te digo que no hay que dejarse enrollar por el viento
Que es necesario llamar a la puerta del torbellino
Nunca debes huir al acercamiento del horror ni de la simple novia que
  canta la alegría de sus arterias
Ningún abismo debe perturbar el reír de los dientes heroicos
Ningún aliento debe empañar el metal de tu alma
Ni remecer tus edificios internos
Quiero verlos brillar siempre con el mismo fósforo del tiempo
Encima del ala viril inmovilizada a causa de su blancura
No esperes ese encuentro prometido en los profundos terciopelos eternos

Without even looking at the drifting king who has forgotten any
    emergency manoeuvres
Like no-one else I have seen open solitude rising beneath my feet
And I have felt the starburst in my eyes
Perhaps the very same one as in unknown locations
Remoteness with no solution
The site high up where someone has left footprints
The extreme tip of the tree where infinity begins
And the sea in the distance like the terror of the night
Silence I beg you all silence
There is a dream that occurs amongst men
There is a dream in progress amongst men and there are portents
We thirst for a place with no restlessness and with no calculation
Where the storm demon will have withered eyes and its hair cut short
Silence I beg you
Watch my soul's hypnotised ship sail by
Dragging a long beard of water
Look at that star in the furthest reaches of the sky
That star leaving with all its sailors

III

We need to throw out numbers and follow them with our eyes
See them take their places seek the unfair puff of smoke
Or even fall into the depths of memory
I tell you do not get caught up in the wind
That one needs to knock on the whirlwind's door
You should never run away from approaching horrors nor from the
    simple bride singing of the joy in her arteries
No abyss should disturb the laughter of your heroic teeth
No breath should tarnish the metal of your soul
Nor make your inner structures shake
I want to see them always blazing with time's same phosphorous
Above the manly wing immobilised because of its whiteness
Do not expect that promised encounter deep in the endless Velvets

Es preciso cubrir el naufragio bajo un edredón de lana
Es preciso saludar los oráculos del mar
Encadenar el paraíso bajo el fuego de nuestra voz
Devolver nuestro corazón a su tienda
No queremos reparticiones gratuitas antes de la vida
Es preciso tapar el naufragio con un corcho cualquiera
Olvidar el vuelo de las manos desesperadas
No hay circunstancias atenuantes para el cielo
Yo no quiero resbalar sobre las nubes ni caer en trampas tendidas por el
        enemigo que no se nombra
Que la muerte desesperada aúlle y que lance su simiente
Que tambalee entre las piedras de sus abismos
Que divida los hombres
Que divida los hombres digo en rangos de sombra y de luz
La insinuación del misterio
La alternativa de dos orillas a escoger
Tampoco así me verás temblar
He aquí el polo sin fin he aquí el mar
He aquí el naufragio bajo una tapa de metal
El naufragio es el plato del cielo
No me verás temblar
Ni aún al ras de la medianoche definitiva
De esa virginal medianoche de todo hombre que nos espera a la orilla
        de nosotros mismos
De esa última medianoche que recae a veces con la quilla en el aire
No me verás temblar
Muy al contrario meceré las sombras en torno mío
Prepararé yo mismo el viento que debo empujarme
El gran viento solitario que quiere abrazar el destino
Tras de la postrera roca en donde se aferra la última sirena fatigada bajo
        el peso de sus cabellos sonoros

He aquí la roca sombrío o primer semáforo del infinito irresistible sólo
        semejante a los ojos del vértigo
He aquí erguida la roca tenebrosa como la estatua del destino
Más allá está la zona sin frente ni cuerpo
La zona amarga como el viento después del rayo

We need to cover the shipwreck with a woollen quilt
We need to greet the sea's oracles
Shackle paradise to our fiery voices
Return our hearts to the shop
We have no wish for free handouts before life begins
We need to plug the shipwreck with an ordinary cork
Forget the flight of desperate hands
There are no extenuating circumstances for the sky
I do not want to trip over clouds or fall into traps set by the enemy who
    shall not be named
May desperate death howl and hurl its seed
May it totter amongst the stones of its chasms
May it divide mankind
May it divide mankind I say ranked by light and shade
The suggestion of mystery
The alternative with two sides to choose from
You will not see me tremble either
Here is the never-ending pole here is the sea
Here is the shipwreck under a metal lid
The shipwreck is heaven's dish
You will not see me tremble
Not even when at the stroke of the final midnight
Of that virginal midnight of mankind that awaits us on the shores of
    our own selves
Of that final midnight that sometimes falls back with its keel in the air
You will not see me tremble
Quite the contrary I will swing the shadows around me
I will prepare the wind myself that I need to push me
The great solitary wind that tries to embrace destiny
Beyond the final rock where the last weary siren clings under the weight
    of her sonorous hair

Here is the gloomy rock or first signal of irresistible infinity just like the
    eyes of vertigo
Here is the dark rock the very image of destiny
Further away is the area with no brow no body
The area bitter as the wind after a lightning strike

La zona vacía en donde una pluma planea desde el principio del mundo
En donde todo se sepulta y se disuelve en el espesor de un manto
      irrisorio que cubre a los mendigos cósmicos
Los mendigos en agonía milenaria que se arrastran atados por la ley
      de las alucinaciones buscando una evidencia

The empty area where a feather has been gliding since the world began
Where everything is buried and dissolves under the mass of a ridiculous
    cloak that concealed cosmic beggars
Beggars in ancient death-throes dragged along by the law of hallucina-
    tions seeking proof

[LA MUERTE QUE ALGUIEN ESPERA]

La muerte que alguien espera
La muerte que alguien aleja
Le muerte que va por el camino
La muerte que viene taciturna
La muerte que enciende las bujías
La muerte que se sienta en la montaña
La muerte que abre la ventana
La muerte que apaga los faroles
La muerte que aprieta la garganta
La muerte que cierra los riñones
La muerte que rompe la cabeza
La muerte que muerde las entrañas
La muerte que no sabe si debe cantar
La muerte que alguien entreabre
La muerte que alguien hace sonreír
La muerte que alguien hace llorar

La muerte que no puede vivir sin nosotros

La muerte que viene al galope del caballo
La muerte que llueve en grandes estampidos

[THE DEATH THAT SOMEONE AWAITS]

The death that someone awaits
The death that someone drives off
The death that is on the way
The death that comes sullenly
The death that lights candles
The death that sits on the mountain
The death that opens the window
The death that extinguishes lanterns
The death that clenches the throat
The death that shuts down the kidneys
The death that breaks one's neck
The death that bites into one's entrails
The death that does not know whether to sing
The death that someone leaves ajar
The death that someone smiles at
The death that someone mourns

The death that cannot live without us

The death that comes galloping on horseback
The death that rains with a great crash

UNA VERSIÓN FRANCESA

UNE VERSION EN FRANÇAIS

A FRENCH VERSION

LE PASSAGER DE SON DESTIN

I

C'est ainsi que nous sommes
Et que nous nous promenons aujourd'hui sur la terre
Précédés par les bruits de nos ancêtres et suivis par la douleur de nos fils
Accrochés à notre âge et chantant quand les rochers pleurent la mort
        d'un voilier qu'ils ont préféré sans aucune raison
Ou peut-être parce qu'ils l'avaient vu jouer dans son enfance
Ou parce qu'il était beau tout rempli de vent venant du pays du vents.
Nous n'avons pas peur que le vent arrache les mots de nos gorges
Nous n'avons pas peur des baleines ni de tous ces monstres qui ont plus
        d'envergure qu'un son de cloche
Nous n'avons pas peur de nous pencher sur vos chansons d'où peut jaillir
        un geyser menaçant et le vertige infini des brumes
Nous n'avons pas peur de l'au-delà qui s'agite comme un muet l'au-delà
        qui va bondir sur nos raisons
Ni de ce froid lucide qui veille sur la constellation de nos soucis
Plus absurde que le mort qu'on a enterré avec la moitié d'une lettre dans
        le cerveau
Avec un mot fabuleux au milieu de la langue
Avec un grand visage entre deux fils de larmes au fond de ses yeux qui
        deviendront de tendres cailloux sur les chemins de l'au-delà

Tout cela est utile à la formation de la surface
À l'intérêt du feu impatient au fond de son antre
Et nous devons signaler son travail et louer sa loi

Il est tard dans tous les coins du monde
Il est tard et le tard va couler dans la mer
Sans lâcher la barre de l'horizon
Car il est le chef unique il détient le secret
Il peut lever le bras et détacher de la mort le cadavre récent.
Maintenant que tu trembles comme la mer

PASSENGER OF HIS DESTINY

1

That is how we are now
And how we walk the earth today
Preceded by the sounds of our ancestors and followed by the sorrow of
    our sons
Clinging to our age and singing while the rocks mourn the death of a
    sailing boat they preferred for no reason at all
Or perhaps it was because they had seen it playing as a child
Or because it was beautiful all full of wind coming from the land of winds.
We are not afraid when the wind blows the words from our throats
We are not afraid of whales or all those monsters whose wingspan is
    greater than a peal of bells
We are not afraid of concentrating on your songs from which a menacing
    geyser and the infinite vertigo of mist might gush forth
We are not afraid of the hereafter fretting like a mute the hereafter that
    will leap over our reason
Nor of that lucid cold that watches over the constellation of our worries
More absurd than the dead man they locked up with half a letter in his
    brain
With one fabulous word at the centre of his tongue
With a great face between two threads of tears deep in his eyes that will
    turn into tender pebbles on the paths of the hereafter

All this is useful for shaping the surface
For interesting the impatient fire deep in its den
And we should mention his work and praise its law

It is late in every corner of the world
It is late and the late afternoon is about to sink into the sea
Without releasing the horizon's rudder
Because it is the sole master it keeps the secret
It can raise an arm and untether fresh corpses from death.
Now that you tremble like the sea

L'horizon va couler pour toujours
Maintenant que la forêt passe à l'ennemi
Écarte les flots comme le cadavre écarte l'éternité
Homme tu vois que la mer se mélange et tu as peur
Tu pourrais bien sauter par-dessus la conflagration des mensonges unanimes
Envahis le terrain sidéral sans hésiter
Envahis les pays du fou qui te méprise et te regarde avec la partie
        inférieure de son âme
Proclame ton importance à la tribu soumise qui commence à apparaître
        au fond du ciel.

II

La terre est en fièvre à cause des chants séculaires des oiseaux
C'est l'inutile réveil de la tribu s'illuminant à chaque pas
La mer lave ses vagues qui doivent le monde
Et répandre leurs caresses jusqu'à la disparition de la contrée
Il est probable qu'elles vont polir le ciel comme la proue d'un grand navire
Peut-être elles vieilliront plus vite que les arbres hantés par les fantômes
        après minuit
Les arbres sans chance les arbres perdus comme l'aïeul qui tente de
        sortir de notre profondeur
Et faire des gestes d'absence dans le vide.
Voici l'événement abrupt après la perdition
Voici l'ordinaire souffrance de celui qui ne peut arrêter les rivières
Et doit pleurer leur mort comme les montagnes
C'est en vain qu'il voudrait clore la mer
Demain les écumes émettront une pensée nouvelle
Feront des couronnes brillantes pour mon cœur capable de rouler ainsi
        que vos meilleurs voiliers
La mémorable catastrophe s'enfuit sans attendre le résultat
Elle s'enfonce à toutes voiles dans les eaux anciennes
Sans même regarder le roi à la dérive qui a oublié les manœuvres d'exception
J'ai vu le premier surgir sous mes pieds la béante solitude
Et j'ai senti dans mes yeux le sursaut stellaire

The horizon is going to sink once and for all
Now that the forest is going over to the enemy
Dividing the waves the way a corpse divides eternity
Man you see that the seas merge and you are afraid
You may as well jump over the conflagration of unanimous lies
Invade the celestial sphere with no hesitation
Invade the lands of the madman who despises you and watches you with
    the lesser part of his soul
Proclaim your importance to the subdued tribe that starts to appear in
    the furthest reaches of the sky.

II

The earth is in a fever because of secular birdsong
It is the useless awakening of the tribe lighting up with every step
The sea washes its waves that should soften the world
And spreads caresses until the land's demise
It is likely they will polish the sky like the prow of a great ship
Perhaps they will age more quickly than the ghost-obsessed trees after
    midnight
The unfortunate trees the trees lost like an ancestor trying to emerge
    from our depths
Making gestures of absence in the void.
Here is the sudden event after the downfall
Here is the usual misfortune of one unable to hold rivers back
Who must mourn their death like the mountains
In vain would he like to seal off the sea
Tomorrow the surf will express a new thought
Will make bright crowns for my heart capable of moving like your finest
    sailing boats
The memorable catastrophe flees without waiting for the result
It sinks under full sail in the ancient waters
Without even looking at the drifting king who has forgotten any
    emergency manoeuvres
I was the first to see the yawning solitude rise up beneath my feet
And I have felt the starburst in my eyes

Le peut-être identique aux parages inconnus
La lointain sans issue le lieu de l'altitude où quelqu'un a laissé l'empreinte
        de ses pieds
La pointe extrême de l'arbre où commence l'infini
Et la mer au loin comme la terreur de la nuit.

Silence je vous pris silence
Il y a un songe qui passe parmi les hommes
Il y a un songe en chemin parmi les hommes et les présages
Nous avons soif d'un lieu sans inquiétude et sans calcul
Où le démon de la tempête aura les yeux flétris et les cheveux coupés
Silence je te prie
Regarde passer la nef hypnotisée de ton âme
Traînant une longue barbe d'eau
Regarde cette étoile au fond du ciel
Cette étoile qui passe avec tous ses matelots

III

Il faut jeter les nombres et les suivre de nos yeux
Les voir prendre leur place chercher l'élévation injuste de la fumée
Ou bien tomber au fond de la mémoire
Je te dis qu'il ne faut pas se laisser enrouler par le vent
Qu'il faut sonner à la porte du tourbillon
Jamais tu ne dois fuir l'approche de l'horreur ni de la simple fiancée qui
        chante la joie de ses artères
Nul gouffre ne doit troubler le rire de tes dents héroïques
Nul souffle ne doit ternir le métal de ton âme
Ni faire branler tes bâtiments internes
Je veux les voir briller toujours avec le même phosphore du temps
Au-dessous de l'aile virile immobilisée à cause de sa blancheur
N'attends pas cette rencontre promise dans les profonds velours éternels
Il nous faut couvrir le naufrage sous un édredon de laine
Il faut saluer les oracles de la mer
Enchaîner le paradis sous le feu de notre voix
Renvoyer notre cœur à sa boutique

Perhaps one identical with parts unknown
The distant dead end the place high up where someone has left footprints
The extreme tip of the tree where infinity begins
And the sea in the distance like the terror of the night.

Silence I beg you all silence
There is a dream that occurs amongst men
There is a dream in progress amongst men and there are portents
We thirst for a place with no restlessness and with no calculation
Where the storm demon will have withered eyes and its hair shorn
Silence I beg you
Watch your soul's hypnotised ship pass by
Dragging a long beard of water
Look at that star in the furthest reaches of the sky
That star passing by with all its sailors

III

We must throw out the numbers and follow them with our eyes
See them take their places seek the unfair puff of smoke
Or even fall into the depths of memory
I tell you do not let the wind get the better of you
You should ring the whirlwind's doorbell
You should never flee from approaching horrors nor the simple bride
       singing of the joy in her arteries
No abyss should disturb the laughter of your heroic teeth
No breath should tarnish the metal of your soul
Nor make your inner structures shake
I want to see them always glowing with time's same phosphorous
Above the manly wing immobilised because of its whiteness
Do not expect that promised encounter deep in the endless Velvets
We will need to cover the shipwreck with a woollen quilt
We will need to greet the sea's oracles
Shackle paradise to our fiery voices
Return our hearts to the shop

Nous ne voulons pas de livraisons gratuites avant la vie
Il faut boucher le naufrage avec un tampon de bois
Oublier l'envol des mains désespérées
Il n'y a pas de circonstances atténuantes pour le ciel
Je ne veux pas glisser sur les nuages ni tomber dans les pièges tendus
      par l'ennemi qu'on ne nomme pas
Que la mort éperdue hurle et qu'elle étale sa semence
Qu'elle chancelle parmi les pierres de ses abîmes
Qu'elle partage les hommes je dis en des rangs d'ombre et de lumière
L'insinuation du mystère
L'alternative de deux bords à choisir
Quand même tu ne me verras pas trembler.
Voici le pôle sans fin voici la mer
Voici le naufrage sous un couvercle d'étain
Car le naufrage est le plat du ciel
Tu ne me verras trembler
Même au ras du minuit définitif de ce vierge minuit de tout homme qui
      nous attends à la rive de nous-mêmes de ce dernier minuit qui
      retombe parfois la coque en l'air
Tu ne me verras pas trembler
Bien au contraire je bercerai les ombres autour de moi
Je préparerai moi-même le vent qui doit me pousser
Le grand vent solitaire qui veut étreindre le destin
Derrière le roc ultime où s'accroche la dernière sirène fatiguée sous le
      poids de ses cheveux sonores
Voici le roc sombre ou premier sémaphore de l'infini irrésistible seul
      semblable aux yeux du vertige
Voici debout le roc ténébreux comme la statue du destin
Plus loin est la zone sans front ni corps
La zone amère comme le vent après la foudre
La zone vide où une plume voltige depuis le premier jour du monde
      où tout s'ensevelit et se dissoud dans l'épaisseur d'un manteau
      dérisoire qui couvre les mendiants cosmiques
Les mendiants en agonie séculaire qui se traînent attachés para la loi des
      hallucinations cherchant une évidence.

We have no wish for free handouts before life begins
We should plug the shipwreck with a wooden stopper
Forget the flight of desperate hands
There are no extenuating circumstances for the sky
I do not want to slip on the clouds or fall into traps set by the enemy
        who shall not be named
Let desperate death howl and spread its seed
Let it totter amongst the stones of its chasms
Let it divide mankind I say ranked by light and shade
The suggestion of mystery
The alternative with two sides to choose from
Even so you will not see me tremble.
Here is the never-ending pole here is the sea
Here is the shipwreck under a tin lid
For the shipwreck is heaven's dish
You will not see me tremble
Not even at the final stroke of this virginal midnight hour midnight of
        mankind waiting for us on the shore of our own selves of that
        final midnight which sometimes falls back with its hull in the air
You will not see me tremble
Quite the contrary I will rock the shadows around me
I will prepare the wind myself that I need to push me
The great solitary wind that tries to embrace destiny
Beyond the final rock where the last weary siren clings under the weight
        of her sonorous hair
Here is the gloomy rock or first signal of an irresistible infinity just like
        the eyes of vertigo
Here stands the dark rock like the statue of destiny
Further away is the area with no brow no body
The area bitter as the wind after a lightning strike
The empty area where a feather has been gliding since the world began
        where everything is buried and is dissolved in the mass of a
        ridiculous cloak that conceals cosmic beggars
Beggars in age-old death-throes dragged along bound by the law of
        hallucinations seeking the obvious.

LA ÚLTIMA ENTREVISTA

THE LAST INTERVIEW

LA COLINA
DEL DESENCANTADO

una entrevista con Jorge Onfray*

Ésta es la casa del poeta. Ésta es su colina, la mágica colina marítima. Y éstos son sus viñedos, éstos sus ondeantes trigos, sus árboles, sus huertas, sus hondonadas ricas de sombra y humedad.

Pero sus fabulosos dominios no se extienden sólo a la hacienda que heredó, amorosamente cultivada trecho a trecho; ni a los campos de frenéticas simientes; ni a los cerros que, cual costras de pan duro, ondulan sobre el litoral: se extiende más allá de la ciudad más allá de las playas; terminan en la línea azul del horizonte. El deseo y el conocimiento son principios de posesión: ¿quién más que el artista puede poseer? ¿Crear no es acaso poseer? Y, ¿quién sino el artífice crea lo que el Señor olvidó crear? El poeta dijo en sus versos:

> Sólo para nosotros viven
> todas las cosas bajo el sol.

> El poeta es un pequeño Dios.

Y, ¿qué es el mar para el poeta, para este Vicente Huidobro, actor y víctima involuntaria de sus obras? Un retablo de olas y algas donde desarrollar sus sueños. Él lo ha dicho también: «El mar puede apenas ser mi teatro en ciertas tardes».

Allí, pues, vive el escritor, en buscado exilio, rodeado de sus seres queridos, visitado por sus discípulos, en la alucinadora tarea de crear, la que comienza leyendo y releyendo, observando, meditando y que concluye componiéndose las febriles estrofas.

Yo creía, en los días de convivencia, que Huidobro se había ya desinteresado de los dilemas humanos y escépticamente dejado de preocupar de dilucidarlos. Seguía como siempre unilateral y violento, tan henchido de ardores: ciego y apasionado en sus ternuras; sonriente, socarrón, en sus odios;

---

* En: *Zig-Zag*, Santiago, 26 de septiembre, 1946, pp. 31-32.

THE DISILLUSIONED MAN ON THE HILL

*an interview with Jorge Onfray**

This is the poet's house. This is his hill, the magical hill on the coast. And these are his vineyards, this is his rustling wheat, his trees, his orchards, his dells rich in shade and humidity.

But his fabulous domains do not extend only to the estate he inherited, lovingly cultivated in places, nor to the fields of frantic seeds, nor to the hills that ripple over the littoral like crusts of stale bread: they extend beyond the city, beyond the beaches; they end at the blue line of the horizon. Desire and knowledge are the fundamentals of possession: who else but the artist can possess them? And who but the craftsman creates what the Lord neglected to create? The poet said in one of his poems:

> Only for us do they live
> all the things under the sun.

> The poet is a little God.

And what is the sea for the poet, for this Vicente Huidobro, actor in – and inadvertent victim of – his works? A tableau of waves and seaweed in which to develop his dreams. He has said so himself: "Some evenings the sea is nothing more than my theatre."

This, then, is the place where the writer lives, in deliberate exile, surrounded by his loved ones, visited by his disciples, engaged in the hallucinatory task of creation, which he begins by reading and rereading, observing, meditating and which he concludes by composing fevered lines of verse.

In the days we spent together, I thought that Huidobro had lost interest in the dilemmas of mankind and, out of scepticism, had ceased to concern himself with their elucidation. He was still as single-minded and forceful as ever, so full of vigour: blind and passionate in his tenderness; smiling, sly

---

* In: *Zig-Zag*, Santiago, 26 September, 1946, pp. 31-32.

encumbrando a los ausentes amigos a inalcanzables alturas, pisoteando con los pies del escarnio y del desprecio a los adversarios; irónico, acre, alerta como nervio excitado, rápido de labia, pronto al cariño y a la burla, suave en la alabanza, implacable en la invectiva. Pero, en apariencia, desvinculado de toda síntesis impersonal, universal. Tal yo creía. Hasta que le sonsaqué las verdades y lloré que me hablara, buscándole, adivinándole los temas preferidos, comprendiendo de fuente directa su limpio amor al hombre y eso que una vez dijo: «El hombre es el hombre y yo soy su profeta».

Mi hazaña de hacerle conversar no era grande, porque el escritor se complace en charlas, en diatribas, en conclusiones dialécticas; y cuando abre la boca, con la facilidad y firmeza de quien tiene algo que transmitir, cuando redondea su opinión, que es siempre un mensaje, alza la voz, los ojos fijos, la boca temblorosa, con exaltación verbal que no admite al auditor duda ni réplica.

Era una tarde de este invierno, tibia y celeste. Yo acompañaba a mi anfitrión por polvorosos senderos que serpeaban entre las malvaviscas mordidas por las liebres. Dejamos atrás el bosque de eucaliptos cenicientos, los sauces y los saúcos, y los aromos con sus pálidas yemas y los grupos de fucsias agitadas por la brisa como campanillas de carnaval. (No sé describir ni enumerar los colores, los perfumes ni el significado de las cosas que nos rodeaban. Y aunque fuera forzoso trazar el marco natural, sería imposible hacerlo porque los olores y los perfumes y el sentido lírico de todo variaban como regalos de cada minuto.)

Curioso era escuchar al poeta, bastón de tallada encina en mano, pistola al cinto, lanzando vibrantes respuestas coreadas por sus negros y olisqueadores perros que nos seguían, ladrando y saltando a nuestras piernas…

La guerra y la poesía

La guerra es el ritornello que tiñe de amargura los labios de Huidobro. Hecho explicable para quien estuvo cuatro terribles años soportando en carne propia y sensibilísima el calor de las masacres, amenazado segundo a segundo por la muerte, la sangre inútilmente vertida, el hedor de los cadáveres, presenciando el pillaje de las ciudades y la violación de las mujeres. Espectáculo bárbaro que trae un execrable e inevitable recuerdo, un nuevo y doloroso modo de asistir a la vida.

¿Hasta qué punto ha cambiado su poética al contacto directo con la experiencia brutal de la guerra? —le pregunté.

in his antipathies; raising absent friends to unattainable heights, trampling his adversaries underfoot with scorn and contempt; ironic, harsh, guarded, like an excited nerve, rapid of speech, quick to affection and mockery, gentle in praise, implacable in invective. But apparently detached from any impersonal, universal synthesis. Or so I thought. Until I coaxed the truth from him and begged him to speak to me, seeking him out, guessing at his favourite topics, understanding from the horse's mouth his clear love of mankind; as he once said, "Man is man and I am his prophet."

Getting him to talk was no great feat, because the writer delights in chatter, in diatribes, in dialectical conclusions; and when he opens his mouth, with the ease and firmness of one who has something to convey, when he sums up his opinion, which is always a message, he raises his voice, eyes fixed, mouth trembling, with a verbal excitement that admits of no doubt or reply from his audience.

It was one afternoon this winter, warm and heavenly. I accompanied my host along dusty paths that wound through hollyhocks nibbled by hares. We left behind us the woods of pale eucalyptus, willows and elder trees, and sweet acacias with their pale buds and clusters of fuchsias waving in the breeze like carnival bells. (I cannot describe or enumerate the colours, the perfumes or the significance of the things that surrounded us. And even if defining the natural setting were unavoidable, it would be impossible to do so because the smells, the scents and the lyrical meaning of it all varied like fleeting treats.)

It was odd listening to the poet, carved oak cane in hand, a pistol in his belt, firing off vibrant responses chorused by the black, snuffling dogs that followed us, barking and jumping around our legs…

War and Poetry

War is the *ritornello* that tinges Huidobro's lips with bitterness. This is understandable for someone who spent four terrible years enduring in person the heat of massacres, threatened every second by death, blood uselessly spilt, the stench of corpses, witnessing the pillaged cities and the violation of women. A barbaric spectacle that carries an execrable and unavoidable memory, a new and painful way of witnessing life.

—*To what extent has direct contact with the brutal experience of war changed your poetics?* I asked him.

Yo mismo no lo sé. Lo único que sé es que me siento más lleno de poesía, de ideas que afirmar, de cosas que decir. Siento un vigor y una plenitud como nunca: un renuevo total.

Vea usted: la guerra produce un desprecio, una desilusión del hombre. Pero al mismo tiempo, una gran ternura por esos niños desvalidos, desorientados, tan ingenuos, que se llaman hombres; un fondo de ternura que se entremezcla constantemente al desprecio haciendo desaparecer todo sentimiento demasiado rotundo.

Cabe preguntarse por qué el nombre de niños se trueca de pronto por el de hombres, y por qué no por el de fantasmas o el de títeres. Los hombres son fantasmas o fantasmones un poco más peligrosos que los niños, porque son actuantes y por esto mismo, más cómicos o más trágicos.

¿Cambia un hombre que ha leído todo Shakespeare, o todo Cervantes, o Pascal, o Montaigne o Dostoyevski? Sí, cambia. Y si a la mayoría nada le pasa es porque no ha comprendido nada.

Muchísimo tiene que transformarnos la guerra. La sangre, los alaridos de dolor, los gritos de rabia, el ruido infernal de los cañones, todo ese drama siniestro, ¿se soporta acaso fácilmente? Claro que sí. Increíble es cómo el hombre se habitúa a todo, pero también es innegable que el horroroso peso de esa visión cotidiana ha de dejar profundas huellas en su espíritu. Pasar días y meses por sobre moribundos tiene que modificarnos; el choque tan acelerado de las sensaciones y de los sentimientos debe forzosamente hacernos variar.

No sólo mi poética sino toda mi persona y mi manera de mirar la existencia y de sentirla tienen que haberse transmutado. Un amigo me decía que la vida ha sido demasiado generosa conmigo y que, en estos tiempos tan artificiales y tan llenos de mediocridad, yo soy uno de los raros poetas con vida de poeta... Yo opino que la mediocridad triunfante ha existido siempre; es natural que así sea porque lo fácil es más asequible que lo difícil. Lo fácil desaparece pronto, pero lo difícil, más duro de masticar, lleva siempre semillas de eternidad.

Panorama actual y futuro

Sin miedo a la bomba atómica, ¿puede traer la paz y acabar definitivamente con las guerras?

No. Lo mismo se dijo hace años a propósito de los gases asfixiantes. Ningún progreso bueno para la guerra lo es para la paz, salvo que los

I really don't know. All I do know is that I feel more filled with poetry, with ideas to be asserted, with things to say. I feel a vigour and a plenty like never before: a complete renewal.

You see, war produces contempt, disillusion in mankind. But at the same time, a great tenderness for those helpless, disoriented, naïve children called mankind; a depth of tenderness that is constantly intermingled with contempt, making all overly forceful feelings disappear.

One wonders why the word *boy* suddenly changes to *man*, and why not to *ghost* or to *puppet*. Men are ghosts or show-offs, a little more dangerous than children because they are actors and, for this reason, more comic or more tragic.

Does a man who has read all of Shakespeare, or all of Cervantes, or Pascal, or Montaigne or Dostoyevsky change? Yes, he changes. And if nothing happens to most of them, it's because they have understood nothing.

There is an overwhelming need for us to transform war. The blood, the screams of pain, the cries of rage, the infernal noise of cannon, all that sinister drama: can anyone easily tolerate it? Of course they can. It is unbelievable how people get used to it all, but it is also undeniable that the horrifying burden of seeing this every day has to have an indelible spiritual effect. Spending days, months on top of dying people has to change us; the accelerated shock of those sensations, of those feelings, must necessarily cause us to change.

Not only my poetics but my whole character and my way of looking at life, and feeling it, must have been altered. A friend told me that life has been too generous to me and that, in this day and age – so artificial and filled with mediocrity – I am one of the rare poets who lives the life of a poet... In my view, triumphant mediocrity has always existed; it is natural that this should be the case, because easy things are more accessible than difficult things. Easy things soon disappear, but difficult things, tougher to chew, always carry the seeds of eternity.

Current and future outlook

Without fearing the atomic bomb, can it bring peace and put an end to war once and for all?

No. The same was said years ago about asphyxiating gas. No progress that is good for war is good for peace, unless men are able to turn it

hombres sean capaces de volverlo al revés completamente. Lo que sería un problema de adelanto espiritual y no material.

Es lamentable que la utilización de la energía atómica haya empezado en el plano bélico. Es una mancha en el destino de la humanidad que nada podrá borrar y que autorizará a nuestros descendientes para mirarnos con muy legitima compasión.

¿Cómo ve usted el panorama del mundo actual y los problemas en que nos debatimos?

El hombre pasa por un mal momento de su historia. El gusano está dentro de su capullo, en una larga noche, devorándose a sí mismo, para luego salir convertido en algo más espiritual, menos grosero.

Desgraciadamente hay demasiadas fuerzas obscuras que se oponen a toda metamorfosis. El primer asunto es que todos los dirigentes políticos son tontos, ciegos, sordos y [oh calamidad], no son mudos.

Se diría que la inteligencia ha emigrado a otros sectores: Ciencia, Poesía, Artes Plásticas, Ingeniería, Arquitectura o Medicina.

Esos angelitos de la política pretenden resolver conflictos del siglo XX con mentalidad del siglo XIX... y de la peor época de esa centuria. Hay que jugar con otro naipe que ellos no conocen. Ya no hay reina de pique, ni as de trébol, ni caballo de copas, ni siete de bastos; los que conocen la nueva baraja no encuentran sitio para sentarse y empezar la nueva gran partida histórica..., a menos que saquen a los otros por la solapa. Paréntesis que será de violencia y confusión en la sala.

Toda esta batahola de vulgaridad nos está desilusionando. El hombre moderno está sufriendo de una especie de vértigo de ausencia: no sabe a quién creer ni en qué creer. Contradicciones y confusionismo lo arrastran a la exasperación; de pronto oiremos la trágica alarma, el «sálvese quien pueda", y entonces veremos un lindo caos. («Sálvese quien pueda» es el título de un acápite en una de mis obras.)

Nunca hubo tanto asco sobre la tierra. Sin embargo, en medio de la desilusión general, jamás ha habido un mayor número de ilusiones particulares. No perdemos la esperanza; deseamos ser mejores y lo seremos, pese a todas nuestras caídas, nuestros tanteos, nuestras vacilaciones.

No obstante, hay todavía quienes creen que esta guerra se hizo para conseguir la supervivencia del mundo más reaccionario y más antihistórico. ¡Cuánto esfuerzo se ha desplegado en perfeccionar los métodos para aplastar al hombre! ¡Cuán poco en desarrollar los que enseñarían a libertarlo, a dignificarlo y elevarlo!

completely the other way around. Which would be a problem of spiritual rather than material progress.

It is regrettable that the use of atomic energy has begun in the area of warfare. This is a stain on the fate of mankind which nothing can erase and which will entitle our descendants to look upon us with well-earned pity.

How do you see the world today and the problems we are facing?

Mankind is going through a bad moment in its history. The worm is inside its cocoon, throughout a long night, devouring itself, only to emerge later as something more spiritual, less coarse.

Unfortunately there are too many dark forces which oppose all change. The first issue is that all political leaders are crazy, blind, deaf and [oh calamity!], they are not mute.

It would seem that intelligence has migrated to other sectors: Science, Poetry, Fine Arts, Engineering, Architecture or Medicine.

Those little angels of politics aim to resolve 20th-century conflicts with a 19th century mentality… and from the worst period of that century. We have to play another card that they do not know. There is no queen of spades, no ace of clubs, no knight of cups, no seven of wands; those who know the new deck cannot find a place to sit and start the great new historical game… unless they haul the others out by their lapels. A parenthesis that will consist of violence and confusion in the room.

All this vulgar hullabaloo is disillusioning us. Modern man is suffering from a kind of vertigo of absence: he does not know whom to believe or what to believe in. Contradictions and confusion drag him into exasperation; suddenly we will hear the tragic alarm, the "every man for himself", and then we will see some fine chaos. ("Every man for himself" is a chapter title in one of my works.)

Never has there been so much disgust on earth. Yet, in the midst of the general disillusion, there has never been a greater number of individual illusions. We do not lose hope; we want to be better, and we will be better, despite all our failures, our tests, our hesitations.

Yet there are still those who believe that this was a war to save the most reactionary and anti-historical world. How much effort has been expended in perfecting ways of crushing mankind! How little in developing what would teach them to liberate, dignify and elevate themselves!

Política, cosa de tontos

¿Concibe usted al poeta en función política?

Lo concibo en función poética, o sea en función de su oficio, que es un oficio largo y difícil y tan absorbente que un espíritu serio no tiene margen para otras ocupaciones que exijan también atención y estudio.

Peligrosa es la absorción de la política. En general los políticos son bastante estúpidos, mentes vulgares sin cultura; están llenos de ambiciones pequeñas y obsesionados por el éxito inmediato; son resbaladizos, tramposos. ¿Qué saben ellos de poesía? Nada: por eso proclamarán a los mediocres y no comprenderán a los realmente superiores. Sólo los poetas semejantes a ellos pueden avenirse con ellos; la mediocridad habla el mismo lenguaje. Casi todos los poetas con una dominante política entregan la dignidad de su profesión, no solamente porque no la comprenden ni la sienten, sino además por razones de arribismo. Tal es el fenómeno corriente.

Las tiendas políticas poseen hoy día un aparato muy bien montado para la propaganda de sus feligreses. Ayer eran los jesuitas los que tenían la más excelente técnica propagandística; ahora, otras sectas y partidos son los herederos de esa técnica. Pero el confusionismo sembrado es momentáneo y a corto plazo.

Se achaca a ciertos bandos de extrema izquierda el monopolio de inflar peleles pseudoartísticos. Pero, ¿puede olvidarse el número de imbéciles literarios que inflaron el nazismo en Alemania y el fascismo en Italia? ¿y a ese señor José María Pemán, el supremo paquidermo de la lengua castellana hinchado por el falangismo hispánico?

¿Cuál es la cuestión vital de nuestro tiempo?

Ésta es una tremenda pregunta que necesitaría muchas páginas para ser contestada.

El mal del siglo, lo repito, es un vértigo de la nada, un vacío que siente el hombre que no tiene fe en nadie ni en ninguna doctrina, y que no puede tenerla porque ni los sujetos que se presentan como dirigentes ni las doctrinas la merecen.

En todas las criaturas verdaderamente conscientes reina un estado de angustia; ningún espíritu se siente cómodo en este ambiente de hoy, tan gaseoso y caótico. Súmanse los desequilibrios hasta formar un desequilibrio total; y no se oye una voz que pueda resolverlos, coagular la catástrofe, presentar una solución tangible y satisfactoria.

Politics, a Fool's Errand

Do you envisage the poet in a political role?

I envisage him in a poetic role, that is, in the role of his profession, which is a long, difficult profession and so absorbing that a serious spirit has no room for other occupations that also demand attention and study.

What is dangerous is absorption in politics. In general, politicians are rather stupid – vulgar minds with no culture; they are full of petty ambitions and obsessed with immediate success; they are slippery, deceitful. What do they know about poetry? Nothing: that is why they will acclaim the mediocre and will not understand those who are really superior. Only poets similar to them can agree with them; mediocrity speaks the same language. Almost all poets with a dominant political view surrender the dignity of their profession, not only because they neither understand nor feel it, but also for reasons of careerism. This is a common phenomenon.

Today's political parties have a very well put-together apparatus for propagandising their congregation. Yesterday it was the Jesuits who had the most excellent propaganda techniques; now, other sects and parties are their heirs. But any confusion sown is momentary and short-term.

Some extreme left-wing factions have been accused of having a monopoly on the attention paid to pseudo-artistic wimps. But can we forget the number of literary imbeciles who puffed up Nazism in Germany, or Fascism in Italy, and that gentleman José María Pemán,* the Castilian language's supreme pachyderm, bloated by Hispanic Falangism?

What is the vital question of our time?

This is a tremendous question which would take many pages to answer.

The evil of the century, I repeat, is a vertigo of nothingness, an emptiness felt by man, who has no faith in any person, or in any doctrine, and who cannot have faith because neither the subjects who present themselves as leaders, nor their doctrines, deserve it.

A state of anguish reigns in all truly conscious creatures; no spirit is comfortable in today's gaseous and chaotic environment. The imbalances add up to an overall imbalance; and one hears no voice capable of resolving them, solidifying the catastrophe, presenting a tangible and satisfactory solution.

---

* Poet and dramatist (1897–1981), and Director of the Royal Spanish Academy on two occasions.

Mi problema, muy personal, se resuelve en vivir en armonía con los seres circundantes y en consagrarme a mi oficio. En poseer el sentido de la grandeza, en construirse uno mismo cada día y en sentir fuertemente esta construcción íntima en tal forma que ella alcance caracteres universales.

Los que han vivido largos años en la desarmonía saben toda la importancia del vivir armónico. Lo conocen y aspiran a ello. Fundamental es establecer en el globo el mayor bienestar posible y la seguridad de todos, no de unos cuantos privilegiados. Se trata de fundar un nuevo idioma que no sea defensivo, temeroso, equívoco, sino firme, sólido, de hombre a hombre, no de tramposo a tramposo.

Los escritores atacarán...

Nos detenemos en una vertiente de cristalinas y delgadas aguas. Huidobro enmudece, admira un rato el cielo que se va poniendo tenue de luz; y, después, se dobla a recoger al borde de la sonora cascada unos hongos gigantes. Y con delectación de abate de la Edad Media, me anticipa los sabores de la próxima cena: la sopa de cebollas, la carne y el vino, los hediondos y magníficos quesos, los postres innumerables.

Vicente, ¿qué ha hecho usted después de haber sufrido el hambre en Europa?

Comer con más ganas que antes.

Y al cabo de una pausa, lo interrogo sorpresivamente: *¿A quiénes deben atacar los escritores?*

A todos los valores falsos que obstruyen el paso de la verdad. A los fanáticos de cualquiera doctrina que entorpezcan la marcha de la libertad. A los esclavos de sus propias pasiones que impidan el desarrollo de la bondad. En una palabra, a todos aquellos en los cuales domina la animalidad de los ancestros primates sobre la razón.

Felizmente hay una favorable reacción. El número de los que despiertan a la realidad aumenta cada vez más. A pesar del odio y de los ataques de la mediocridad, a pesar de las negras intrigas de todas las cofradías de izquierda o de derecha, a pesar de todos los «esclavos de la consigna», la luz seguirá creciendo y aumentando su calor vivificante dentro del cerebro humano para equilibrar a la tierra que se enfría.

My problem, and it is a very personal one, comes down to living in harmony with those around me and devoting myself to my profession. In possessing a sense of grandeur, in building oneself up every day and having a strong feeling for this intimate edifice such that it attains universal characteristics.

Those who have lived for many years in disharmony know the complete importance of a harmonious existence. They know it and aspire to it. It is essential to establish in this world the greatest possible well-being and security for all, not just for the privileged few. It is a question of establishing a new language which is not defensive, fearful, equivocal, but firm, solid, man to man, not cheat to cheat.

WRITERS WILL ATTACK…

We stop at a stream of fine, crystalline water. Huidobro falls silent, admires the fading sky for a while, and then bends down to pick some giant mush-rooms at the edge of the echoing waterfall. And with all the joy of a medieval priest, he predicts for me the flavours of our next dinner: onion soup, meat and wine, magnificent stinking cheeses, innumerable desserts.

Vicente, what did you do after suffering hunger in Europe?

Eat more eagerly than before.

And after a pause, I ask him unexpectedly: *Whom should writers be attacking?*

All false values that obstruct the passage of truth. The fanatics of any doctrine that hinders the progress of freedom. Those who are slaves to their own passions and who hinder the development of goodness. In a word, all those in whom the bestiality of their primate ancestors takes primacy over reason.

Happily, there has been a favourable reaction. The number of those waking up to reality increases all the time. In spite of the antipathy and attacks by mediocrities, in spite of dark intrigues by all the confraternities of left or right, in spite of all the "slaves of the slogan", the light will continue to grow and increase its life-giving warmth within the human mind so as to balance the cooling earth.

Los falsos valores levantados por conveniencias del momento van desinflándose con rapidez pasmosa. Un amigo me declaraba el año pasado, en París: «Si Paul Éluard, obligado por consignas, declarara que Félix Potin o el pequeño Picetti eran grandes poetas, nadie le creería. Todos nos reiríamos. Hace algún tiempo, muchos jóvenes lo habrían tomado en serio». Esto es exacto. La seriedad va imponiéndose.

La última etapa

He leído en un periódico inglés que a usted lo colocan, junto con André Breton, Paul Éluard y Eliot, entre los más grandes poetas de esta era. ¿Qué piensa usted de ellos? ¿Qué artistas prefiere?

Breton es un hombre de inteligencia asombrosa; hablé mucho con él, últimamente, en Nueva York; es uno de los pocos que no han decaído en absoluto en la hecatombe intelectual paralela a la guerrera. Es un poeta de verdad.

En cambio, Eliot es un mediocre, un pequeño Claudel pueblerino y latero. Me gusta Hans Arp, el único con quien he escrito un libro entero; me gustan René Daumal, que murió durante la guerra; Jacques Prévert que era para mí un gran oasis de poesía y cordura, y Henri Michaux y Ribemont-Dessaignes. En resumen, mis amigos del corazón y los que más frecuenté en los días en que iba a París con permiso desde el frente.

¿Cuál es su última etapa poética?

Me referiré primero a la penúltima, a los libros nacidos en la guerra.

Uno se llama *Sin días y sin noches*, y trata principalmente de esa sensación de estar fuera del tiempo que yo experimenté, sobre todo al final del conflicto. Otro se llama *Utilidad de las estrellas*, y se refiere a la sensación de verse protegido o guiado por un destino especial, como defendido por la misma poesía cual un hijo inválido por su madre. El tercero es un libro de poemas que titulé *El precio del alba* (anunciado ya hace más de un año en Francia y en el Uruguay). Estos poemas muestran el precio que yo he pagado –y que fue casi mi vida– por un renacimiento espiritual completo, por la plenitud, por la renovación absoluta de mi ser.

False values, raised in the expediency of the moment, are collapsing with astonishing speed. A friend of mine told me last year in Paris: "If Paul Éluard, at some commissar's behest, were to declare that Félix Potin* or little Picetti were great poets, nobody would believe him. We would all laugh. A while ago, many young people would have taken him seriously." This is accurate. Seriousness is gaining ground.

The Most Recent Phase

I read in an English newspaper that, along with André Breton, Paul Éluard and Eliot, you are ranked among the greatest poets of this era. What do you think of them? Which artists do you prefer?

Breton is a man of astonishing intelligence; I spoke a great deal with him lately in New York; he is one of the few who has not decayed at all in the intellectual catastrophe that ran alongside the military one. He is a real poet.

Eliot, on the other hand, is a mediocrity, a small-town, backwoods Claudel. I like Hans Arp, the only one with whom I ever wrote a whole book; I like René Daumal, who died during the war; Jacques Prévert, who was for me a great oasis of poetry and sanity, and Henri Michaux and Ribemont-Dessaignes. In short, friends of my heart and the ones I saw during those days when I was in Paris on leave from the front.

What is the most recent phase in your poetry?

I will refer first to the penultimate phase, to the books born during the war.

One is called *Without Days and Without Nights*, and concerns mainly that feeling I experienced of being outside time, above all at the end of the conflict. Another is called *Utility of Stars*, referring to the feeling of being protected or guided by a special destiny, as if defended by poetry itself like an invalid son by his mother. The third is a book of poems which I titled *The Price of Dawn* (announced more than a year ago in France and Uruguay). These poems demonstrate the price I have paid – and it almost *was* my life – for a complete spiritual rebirth, for repletion, for the absolute renewal of my being.

---

* Potin (1820–1871) was a famous retailer in 19th-century France. Woolworth's would be a comparable business. I confess I'm not sure of the identity of Picetti. [Translator]

Respecto a la última etapa, puedo adelantarle que ella se compone de poemitas en un tono muy diferente, quizás con algún parentesco con *Tout à coup*. Algunos que han leído esos versos inéditos los encuentran demasiado desprendidos o desencarnados. Tal vez lo sean. En todo caso, obedecen a un momento muy primordial de mi vida.

* * *

Pronunciadas estas frases con timbre grave y sereno, el poeta se envuelve en hondas reflexiones.

En lo alto de la colina, destacándose en el crepúsculo, surgen las ágiles siluetas de su esposa y de su hijo. Lo llaman insistentemente, y él, sacudiendo las dulciamargas ideas, alegrado de súbito, acude a los frescos clamores.

Yo permanezco solo y pienso: Huidobro es la imagen del desencantado. De un raro desencantado.

No cree como antaño, con entusiasmo, abiertamente, en los prodigios del género humano. Mas, no se desespera. Y busca nuevas y apacibles fórmulas de luchar por ese bien que les está faltando a los hombres.

No quiere que le sigan prosélitos ni se ilusiona en una virtud contagiosa de sus lecciones. Él dice una verdad que a todos alcanza, que habíamos olvidado, pero inesperada y muy amplia. Y eso le basta.

As for the most recent phase, I can tell you that it consists of short poems in a very different tone, perhaps with some resemblance to *Tout à coup*.* Some who have read these unpublished verses find them too detached or disembodied. Perhaps they are. In any case, they are a response to a very vital moment in my life.

* * *

These phrases are uttered in a low, serene tone, and the poet becomes deeply thoughtful.

At the top of the hill, standing out in the twilight, the lithe silhouettes of his wife and son emerge. They keep calling him and he, shaking off any bitter-sweet thoughts, suddenly cheers up and heeds their renewed cries.

I remain alone and think: Huidobro is the very image of a disillusioned man. An uncommonly disillusioned man.

He does not believe as he once did, enthusiastically, openly, in the wonder of the human race. But he does not despair. And he seeks new and peaceful ways to fight for the good that is lacking in mankind.

He seeks no disciples to follow him, nor does he delude himself that his lessons might have some contagious virtue. He speaks a truth that reaches everyone, one that we have forgotten, but also one which is both unexpected and very comprehensive. And that is enough for him.

---

* *Tout à coup* [All of a Sudden] was a book of poems in French, published by Huidobro in 1925. The Shearsman collection, *Paris 1925*, includes the full text together with another French volume from the same year.

NOTES

Prior publication of the poems in this volume occurred as follows. All titles not mentioned were first collected in the 1948 first edition of *Últimos poemas* (UP1948).

Antología, 1935, is the *Antología de poesía chilena nueva* [Anthology of New Chilean Poetry], edited by Eduardo Anguita and Volodia Teitelboim, published in Santiago in 1935; *Antología*, 1945, is a Selected Works – mainly poetry – edited for Ediciones Zig-Zag, Santiago, by Eduardo Anguita in 1945, the last major collection of his work before the author's death. OP2003 is the *Obra poética*, ed. Cedomil Goic (2003), the most authoritative compendium of Huidobro's poetry to date. UP2012 is the edition of *Últimos poemas* published by the Fundación Huidobro in Santiago. PR2021 is the *Poesía reunida* (ed. Vicente Undurraga, Santiago: Editorial Lumen, 2021).

'El paso del retorno'
Amargo 3, Santiago, December 1946. Published with a date of September 1945, and a footnote to the effect that it had been read on Radio "Espectador", Montevideo, in October 1945. The original magazine publication included a dedication to Huidobro's partner, Raquel Señoret: "A Raquel, que me dijo un día: Cuando tú te alejas un solo instante, el tiempo y yo lloramos." [To Raquel, who said to me one day: When you go away for a single moment, both time and I weep."]

'Voz de esperanza' — *Multitud* 1:26, Santiago, 1 July 1939.

'Monumento al mar' — *Sur* 7.32, Buenos Aires, May 1937 / *Antología*, 1945.

'Ilusiones perdidas' — *Romance* 1:14, Mexico, 15 August 1940.

'Edad negra' — *Babel*, Santiago, 1940; *Cuadernos Americanos* 3:14, 2, Mexico, March / April 1944; *Antología*, 1945.

'Sea como sea' — *Romance* 1:14, Mexico, 15 August 1940.

'Cambio al horizonte' — *Multitud* 1:12, Santiago, March 1939.

'De cuando en cuando' — *Mandrágora* 1, Santiago, 1938.

'Bellas promesas' — *Mandrágora* 2, Santiago, 1939; *Romance* 1:14, Mexico City, 15 August 1940.

'La mano del instante' — *Mandrágora* 3, Santiago, December 1939.

'Estrella hija de estrella' — The manuscript of this poem carries a dedication to Sylvia Luz Balmaceda (1913–?), the daughter of Teresa Wilms Montt.

'Palabras de la danza' — *Cuadernos Americanos* 3:14, 2, Mexico, March / April 1944, under the title 'Una mujer baila sus sueños' [A Woman Dances Her Dreams].

'El pasajero de su destino' — *Sur* 3.8, Buenos Aires, 1933 / *Antología*, 1935.

'Le passager de son destin' — *Les Feuillets de «Sagesse», collection anthologique,* nº 48, Paris (Éditions Sagesse, au Librairie Tschann, Paris, 1937). This was a *plaquette*, or chapbook, of 8 pages, containing only this poem. The text here is from the original edition on which is printed, below the title, [Fragment]. The original edition does not employ indented carry-overs for long lines, but we have altered that here, in accordance with the author's customary practice, and it also retains a few full-stops at line-ends. While I suspect that those would have been removed by the author, had the text been republished under his supervision, I have opted to retain them here. The publisher was a bookshop at 48, Boulevard Montparnasse. It still exists, but is now at Nº 125, and still specialises in poetry.

The interview with Jorge Onfray was published in the journal *Zig-Zag*, Santiago, 26 September, 1946, pp. 31-32. The text here is drawn from *Textos inéditos y dispersos*, edited by José Alberto de la Fuente Arancibia [1993], Santiago: Ediciones Tácitas. 3rd edition, 2015.

TEXTUAL COMMENTARY

'Una noche momentánea' (pp. 52-61)
Sur le pont d'Avignon / On ne danse plus en rond is a variation on a traditional song, dating back to the 15th century, about the dance performed on the bridge at Avignon. In reality the dance took place under the bridge, so it ought to be *sous*, and not *sur* le pont. The text of the song is "Sur le Pont d'Avignon / L'on y danse, l'on y danse / Sur le Pont d'Avignon / L'on y danse tous en rond." Huidobro's version has the dance no longer taking place, a symbol of France having fallen.

le temps de cerises / Oh bergère bergère rentre tes noirs moutons:
The first phrase [= 'The Time of Cherries'] is a popular song from 1866 that became a favourite of the revolutionary *communards*. The second phrase is a variation on "Il pleut, il pleut bergère / Rentre tes blancs moutons" [It's raining, it's raining, shepherd, / bring back your white sheep], the sheep becoming black in Huidobro's version, and the shepherd becoming female, perhaps France herself, anthropomorphised. The text is from a song in the comic opera *Laure et Pétrarque* [Laura and Petrarch] by Fabre d'Églantine (1780), to music by Louis-Victor Simon.

Finally, the *Carmagnole*, mentioned at the end, is the name of a song and dance that were popular during the French Revolution, and is named after the outfit worn by the revolutionaries – bolero jacket, trousers, sash and red "liberty" cap. Here the author is hoping to dance and sing when victory comes.

'Una tarde después del Rhin' (p.66-69)
Rhin is actually French for the River Rhine. The Spanish name for it is *Rin*. The French name is used in all editions I have consulted and thus it has been retained here.

'Una noche de campos profundos' (p. 96-97)
This is clearly a separate, untitled, text in UP1948, and is again presented as such in UP2012, and PR2021. In OP2003 it has been attached to the end of the previous poem, as though it were a continuation of the final stanza.

While there are mercifully few errors in OP2003, considering the scale of the book, most of those that I *have* found consist of layout and lineation errors, and also a curiously erratic approach to the indentation of carried-over lines. 'Coronación de la muerte' (pp.24-27) is a case in point: UP1948 uses indented carry-overs, whereas OP2003 simply moves the carry-over to start flush with the left margin, using lower-case for the first word carried over, which was emphatically not the author's practice. OP2003 also presents the poems in a different order, and conflates them with uncollected pieces which we will include in a separate volume later in this series.

UP1948 also has an erratic approach to punctuation, seemingly introducing punctuation wherever the editor(s) thought it appropriate. OP2003, after consultation of the manuscripts, eliminates all such punctuation which, again, does reflect the author's practice in his later years, as is quite clear from the two volumes he published in 1941. Our approach here is to present the texts as accurately as we can, and we have adopted the original running-order from UP1948, but with the orthography and (mostly non-)punctuation of OP2003. This approach is validated by the most recent major Spanish-language edition, PR2021, which is the most comprehensive edition of the author's poetry currently in print, despite its signal lack of editorial apparatus and its failure to include *any* of the author's French poems, even where his own translations were available.

www.ingramcontent.com/pod-product-compliance
Lightning Source LLC
Chambersburg PA
CBHW032145160426
43197CB00008B/774